"Janne's fearlessness, no
is what consistently dra
only the brave ones da
writer, another woman cr.   ....
way challenges me to continue to expand my edges, until
there is no truth left untold."
—*LeAnn Rimes, Grammy award-winning singer/songwriter*

"Janne's work is born from deep sensitivity and strength.
In these pages she speaks for women whose voices aren't
heard, at the same time challenging us all to come into our
own power and speak for ourselves. It is bold, direct, and
empowering. It provokes us in order to uplift. If you are
ready to 'stare into the magnificence of all that you are,' it is
time for you to read 'There's cobwebs on her vagina.'"
—*Laurel Sprengelmeyer, singer/songwriter*

"These poems shine brightly and speak loudly, unwavering in
their pursuit of truth and humanity. Janne Robinson writes
from the depths of her soul. And the world is better for it."
—*Alex Banayan, best-selling Author of The Third Door*

"Janne is a unique and powerful voice for poetry. Her hon-
esty and raw vulnerability shines through every poem and
inspires the reader to delve deeper. She is unapologetic. She
is fierce. And she is real. She puts a mirror up to herself
and humanity through her life and her art."
—*IN-Q, National Poetry Slam Champion*

"Reading this book, I had to keep stopping to write down
my own poems of revelation and understanding. Each line
and idea sparked truths within myself. It made me feel like I

could be honest with myself. I could finally come clean about loads of emotions and thoughts I had subconsciously chosen to pretend didn't exist. It was lovely to find them, to nurture them, be inspired by them and then to be grateful they exist."
—*Kim Churchill, National Youth Folk Artist of the Year (2009)*

"Fuck, I feel so powerful and validated when I read Janne's poetry. You know exactly what she's talking about, yet we're never courageous to say it. She says it for all of us boldly and courageously. Janne is a wild Mustang, let's let her words roam free."
—*Suzy Batiz, Founder of Poo-Pourri and Supernatural, Forbes richest self-made woman in America (2019)*

"Janne's words are arrow-sharp, unpolished, and staring at you from the page head-on. She asks for no mercy and takes no bullshit. In a world full of women coming into themselves and stepping into the center, she offers her story boldly and inspires many."
—*Chloe Smith, Rising Appalachia*

"It is rare to feel both deep vulnerability and such grounded strength in the shape and form of words. And it is a gift to witness someone uncover their heart and mind in the ways Janne Robinson has in her expressions. We get to see the world through her eyes, one laced in sensuality at moments, and explore a landscape of her experiences and her movement through them. She has a finger gently on the feminine divine, while also deeply addressing our humanness as a whole, in both our places of beauty and also in the spaces in which we all lean for growth and expansion. This rawness and strength shared in honest snapshots of experience and dreamlike recreations ultimately stands as a mirror for us all to explore our own hearts and minds more deeply, and a catalyst to search for the closer innate connection we have with our bodies, our spirits, our questions, our beings. Naturally, when we explore this, it also becomes the connecting thread that joins us all. Made of the same essences, thoughts and feelings, we experience this world of ours individually, but ultimately in togetherness, in all of its rugged, raw, and fallible beauty."

—*RY X, singer/songwriter*

"Janne's words are courage. She tears down censorship and leaves the filters to the cookie-cutter coffee bean voices, putting her heart and mind on full display in this collection. It's a bold brew that will leave grains of thought stuck in your teeth, and they'll stay there until you floss the topic with the attention it requires. Like a child that runs freely naked before it is shamed, Janne's heart sunbathes in its birthday suit, fully aware that others will point and judge at the way it beats so willingly. That's courage."

—*Gino Anthony Pesi, actor/producer*

"Janne's writing touches places in my psyche I didn't know exist. I feel delicate, subtle stirrings, not easily recognizable—they need attention. Her words convey feelings that have nothing to do with the intellect. She is a wild palomino in a corral—longing, craving to be put out on the prairies. To gallop free, alone, with the rush of wind ruffling her mane. Taking on the whole planet single-handed. Then again there's this other side of her—demure, daintily nibbling at the grass, graceful and calm, enthralled by a red dragonfly on a dry twig. Janne does give a fuck! It's the world around her that doesn't, that can't, because it takes brass cojones to do so."

—*Prem*

THERE'S

COBWEBS

ON HER VAGINA

A COLLECTION OF POEMS BY
JANNE ROBINSON

```
THIS IS
FOR THE
WOMEN
```

Copyright © 2020 Janne Robinson

ALL RIGHTS RESERVED
No part of this book may be translated, used, or reproduced in any form
or by any means, in whole or in part, electronic or mechanical, includ-
ing photocopying, recording, taping, or by any information storage or
retrieval system without express written permission from the author or
the publisher, except for the use in brief quotations within critical articles
and reviews.

Printed and bound in the United States of America

ISBN: 978-1-7340421-0-8

Cover design by Waseema Petersen
Interior layout by Stefan Merour

The poem *There's Cobwebs on Her Vagina* was initially published by
Thought Catalog in *This Is for the Women Who Don't Give a Fuck* and is
reprinted here with permission.

"Trying to be a man is a waste of a woman."

—Allison Pearson

If you woke up today and didn't feel like there was space for you in this world because you were born a woman, then this book is dedicated to you.

Being a woman is the biggest gift bestowed upon us—never forget that.

And if you forget it—come back here to remember.

THERE'S COBWEBS ON HER VAGINA

the gynecologist replies

removing his head from between her freckled thighs

her mother chokes on the air

p—pardon?

It's from a society that shames women for enjoying sex

one that puts purity rings on their fingers

promises them away to God

away from pleasure

pleasure is shameful

you hear?

God is the only one that loves you

What if the husband is a jackrabbit?

what if he lacks all there is to know about making a
woman moan?

what if she dies not having her soul ripple?

her body shake

fall apart

from the hands and tongue of a man who has done his work

a lover of all things woman

God, what if he's gay?

what if he wishes to be making love to a man?

heaven forbid her body is never touched with the tenderness

that we deserve from the moment we are born

It's from a society that throws half-naked sexualized women in
sunglasses commercials making us hide our daughters' eyes

while the men smoking Cuban cigars laugh

making millions off the easiest marketing idea invented

the female body is the greatest piece of art

of course it sells

Shame on us for giving it away

then playing the victims

the big bad media wolves

forcing our hands to paper to sign

there are no victims here

women, are to blame

It's from a society that shrieks at nipples

turns away

they're the same as mine

but

but

they're sexual!

Put them away

I can feel the breeze on my sweltering chest in August

but

you

must

cover

yours

It's from a society that cuts off women's genitals

doesn't give them the right to vote

to work

to live

to love who they choose

covers them in clothes

no, not to hide them from the sun

Marries them away at fourteen

to a twenty-one-year-old called Jose

who drinks four bottles of whisky a day

who falls asleep drunk after they have sex each night

boring

missionary sex

with no foreplay

while she speaks quietly into the night of wanting to be
a lawyer

of how she would bring justice with all her might

He closes her legs

the mother's mouth is still dropped

masturbation, 2 times a day—3 if needed

his white coat wisps behind him as the door shuts

Oh mamma

the world we live in is changing.

HOME IS A PLACE IN MY BELLY

deep

deep down

a place you've never seen

and might never know

my thighs are like mountains

my heart, Jupiter

I carry the planes of the prairies in the lines of my skin

there are wells of power that shake inside of me

you are a visitor

driving upon my land

Don't think you have been offered a seat at my table

until I have pulled you out a chair

don't think you deserve the sustainability of my heartbeat

or the wetness in my thighs just because you offered to
drive

Baby, I grew the seeds of the forest here

we speak the same language

when I walk amongst them

they bend down and whisper of the women you treated
kindly

and the ones you did not

I am the sacredness that only the sunrise and the sunset
can understand

you are a visitor

walking amongst my jungle

don't pick anything

without my permission

you only have permission to watch

Do you see how I walk with this earth?

and not on her?

watch again

for men have been raping and pillaging these lands for
longer than I can understand

taking

rather than asking

now you must earn a seat at my table

for Mother Earth is through with you

and I am too

You are a visitor

don't you understand?

Are you a man-eater?

he asks

I only eat the men

who don't respect me.

TO THE WOMEN WHO ARE THREATENED BY ME

who make ultimatums to the ones they love

me or her

and they choose you

Great

They are enabling your non-growth

they are enabling your insecurity to grow like weeds in the
garden I had in Edmonton

where the green flowed and flowed

because no one did the work

no one got on their knees

in the dirt of what made them uncomfortable

and looked at their shit

Your insecurity isn't about me

you are not threatened by me

You are threatened because you have yet to stare into the
magnificence of all that you are

you have yet to look yourself in the eye of your heart and
see that you are the catch

You are the body he wishes next to him

the lips he wishes to ravish

the heart he wishes to stand upon and proclaim

Yes!

I find it threatening that you take away the freedom from

the one that you love

that you keep him from those that nourish his spirit

the ones that are there

And if I was less sugar and more spice

if I wanted to fuck him

I would have

there was plenty of time for that

If I wanted to take the flesh of him into my lips

I would have

If I wanted to lie him down and taste his sweat

I would have

And maybe I already did

and we decided that the dance wasn't with our limbs or
red hearts

but one of joy

laughter

play

It isn't real

that fear

growing inside your head

I am not your threat

I am a mirror to the excellence inside your spirit

you have yet to stand inside and look up into this world

with eyes like fire and a laugh like honey

a power in your belly that cackles like the witches that live in the fires of those who believe in magic

You will continue to walk with rose-colored glasses until you tap into the love that is inside your heart

like sap

letting it drip upon each inch of your soul until you know for certain that you are all that you need and all that he needs

And then, I may walk into a room

And we may smile—for I am you and you are me

And we share the same truth between our souls.

I AM DIVINE AND YET I TREMBLE

I speak from my heart

of an insecurity that I wish didn't fall from my eyes

my eyes like sunshine

my eyes like God

my heart that encapsulates this entire world

my body that breaks the heart of those that are blind

my mind that frees those who cannot find the words that
speak

I am divine and yet I tremble

For we are new

and she is beautiful

and I feel this tightness in my chest whenever he says her
name

and it terrifies me

so he holds me

and I say it out loud

I brace myself

and he tells me that at one point yes

he did like her

that maybe in another life they did the dance

but not this one

and all of me squirms

squirms because this is the one that I want

and someday

with or without me

he could want her

and hold her like he holds me tonight

and that makes my confidence and strength break like
china inside my heart

That this man

these arms

this love could go away

and it's silly

as there are many I've the same story

many you've the same story

yet there are some who tower like large trees with dark
branches and large shadows

like they could eat us

eat me alive

she is not a threat

yet she is threatening

and I shake in my magnificent heart's boots

disdainful of the fear running through me

terrified that in showing my insecurity he will turn away

insecurity and jealousy are not badges of honor while
dating

these are not the bright bits of myself I have pride in

this is the darkness

and this is my work

for there will be hordes of beautiful women with eyes for

this one's sparkle

hordes

he has a heart the size of Texas

and loves wholly and deeply those around him

he's one of the most tender and beautiful men I've ever
met

I am drowning in being inside of his arms

in the feeling of his full heartbeat

this one is special

I've already seen the ones who see his sparkle

and shaken

It will be my job

to continuously see my light

And know that compatibility is a concoction of so many
things

so many things he and I share

and that ultimately

it's just a choice

that either of us could wake up and walk outside and
choose 10 other people

but that we don't want those 10 other people

that we want each other

that we choose each other

I wish to rest into that so deeply

so this shaking inside my soul unjustly may leave us both

and even if they someday love one another

and it's in this life

there are so many women who have loved him

and may love him

in this life

they all made him this man I want to consume like passion fruit gelato on a 30-degree day on a dock in the summertime

I must be grateful for them all

the ones who have, haven't, and maybe will

How terrifying

it is

to be hit with the impermanence before you've even fallen in love with someone

To be gripped by goingness

To experience the lust of losing someone

just as you're falling into and discovering all of who they are

Yet I know to live in our walk and shake of future women is nonsensical and insulting to presence

our presence

and our time

my presence is like sunshine

I know this

Remember your light

a small voice says

I am the light

I am the light

I close my eyes and try to quiet my heart that beats like a thousand black horses across the Arizona desert

Who's on the couch?

he says

with eyes that glimmer

I shrug and squiggle into him

you're on the couch

he says

kissing me deeply

I receive him

and I receive it each time he says it the next 24 hours

in it I hear

I choose you

I choose you

I choose you

rolling over in bed the next day

I choose you

driving to the airport

I choose you

I choose you too

now I must so deeply choose myself that we could be in a room full of divine, loving, playful, successful, beautiful women

and I do not shake

but smile

because I am one of them

and we are here together

This is my work, darling—and although I love your arms
and affirmation

this is my work to do

I am the light

I am the light

I am the light.

THAT'S WHY WE SHOULD GO EXTINCT

I stand at the checkout line

4 years ago with my old boss

he throws a fit over honey in a plastic cup

why do you have to use plastic?

he pushes it back over the counter

making a scene

in his tall character

red hair

broad chest

I hate confrontation, and my cheeks flush red, and I am embarrassed to be with him

Now

Mother Earth is not just asking

but crying for advocacy

her screams are so loud that they wake us in each corner of the earth at night

natural disaster

after natural disaster

yet when I walk into a coffee shop in liberal California and ask for a coffee to stay I'm handed a disposable cup

I sigh

you don't have to-stay mugs?

I ask

she is bright and cheery, and I don't mean to shit on her

but we're shitting on our planet

No

we don't have a dishwasher

she replies

I look around and see brown disposable mugs everywhere

I am blinded by the waste

and all of a sudden I hear her

Screaming

from the core of lava

she is reaching up

pulling at each of us

scratching her eyes and face

as she yells

STOP!

you're hurting me

you're hurting me

STOP

And yet we are walking, dumping, waste machines

throwing garbage on her earth

sixty percent of species have gone extinct in the last forty
years

our children's children may never see a sea otter

orcas may become the dinosaurs of the past

our children will look at books full of the animals you and
I grew up with

and we will say

yes, sweetie—that one's extinct
and they will look up
with broad brown eyes wide
why mommy?
what happened?

And I will tell her that you and I
were too lazy to bring reusable mugs to coffee shops
that coffee shops didn't give a fuck
that restaurants got styrofoam for cheaper
and they didn't see it standing, piling in dumps
in our oceans
getting in the gills of fish that won't live to see another day
or do
and we eat them
full of our shit and our waste

For we are cutting off our ears as we refuse to recycle
because we're too lazy
because it's too much work
while Mother Earth cries below our feet
they don't care
they don't see
for you and I, we walk upon this earth
and not with her
and that's why we should go extinct.

I AM NOT GAS STATION COFFEE

I am not gas station coffee; I am the orange pottery mug that you love, that you've always owned—filled with coffee from beans that you grind in your kitchen.

Your kitchen that sees the morning light just right—the one that understands what your footsteps say, as though they are speaking to the walls of how you slept.

I am flesh and bones sewn from the ancient groves of these forests—I ran here in the darkness while you were still asleep.

I am composed of spider webs that hold the grey of rain. I am dew glistening on vibrant green. I am silver skies and raindrops that meet the white of the ocean below.

I don't identify with what you identify me with—I am spirit, spirit that runs and plays, laughing through fields at dusk, running her hands through the sweetness of wheat and purple of lavender.

I encompass the heavens inside my chest, the dripping redness of sap that you couldn't shake if you tried.

I have the legs of mountains and the call of an eagle's cry.

I roamed this earth before you began, and I birthed you and everything you are.

Do not come to lap water at my feet if you do not intend to build a home inside the walls of my heart, for I know now what I am, and what I am is sacred.

I THREW ALL MY NEEDS OUT THE WINDOW TODAY
like litter
and they shrieked as they hit the cement
what are you doing?
they called
why?
I was so busy stretching my hands wide to hold you
all day
you
you
you
I didn't have time to think about me
you were in the front dash and rearview mirror
because that's loving, right?
and then suddenly I realize I'm forgetting something
something important
the day has been fine
I survived
but there's something I'm forgetting
it's important
and I know it quite well
me
me
me
I slam on the brakes
I smell burnt black rubber on pavement

tires burning in the Arizona sun

dead-stopped in the desert

I am alone

it is quiet

it is silent

I suddenly hear myself screaming and crying

far

far away

I move the gear stick into reverse

and put my foot on the gas

streamlining at a hundred and forty miles an hour,
backward down the freeway

I see them

my needs

scattered there

I slam on the brakes

slam the red car door

so hard it shakes the earth of everything I am and have
forgotten

no!

I shout

no!

if loving you means abandoning me
I don't choose you anymore

I pick up each one of my needs off the highway

apologizing to them softly

holding their bruises

holding their faces to the sun

they do not forgive me

or trust me

they are in shock

Who says you won't just toss us to the road for the next guy who shows up?

why should we believe that you finally know you better?

I look at them

fear and distrust in their eyes

guarded

you won't

but realizing you've fallen off the horse is the first step to getting back on

and I'm here

aren't I?

and I'm choosing you

I'm choosing me

I'm choosing us

aren't I?

they soften

and hopefully I'll get so good at knowing my needs

that men who ask me to abandon them won't even show their face at my door

that I won't need to choose my needs or their needs

because without it being said, they will be met

we will all be met

they nod

they soften into my hands

thank you

they say

I take three large strides to my car

close the door and get in

turn the radio on to some blues tune by someone with a voice hoarse like honey

and we go.

THE RED DRAGON

We pull up to the side of the yellow dunes

American flags race

dust flies

we have 30 minutes to make it for the shot

we look left

see a man in a red shirt

holding a Corona

I turn to Garrett

unroll your window

let's ask him if it's safe

he walks over

you guys gonna need a flag if you're going in there

we start asking him questions

could you take us?

I ask

sure

he replies

let me grab my wife

one more thing

he's going to photograph me

and

I'm going to be naked

I have four daughters

I won't look

he says

we walk towards the Red Dragon

its sides gleaming in the Californian sun

when you step in there, be careful of the seatbelt so it doesn't scratch the side

I get in

observing five straps

suddenly realizing what we've gotten ourselves into

but not even slightly aware of what we've committed to

I strap in five belts

like a fucking roller coaster

he puts a headset on me with black headphones as big as my head

he turns to me

you can strap him in, right?

my eyes bug bigger than the buggy

and then we're off at what feels like a hundred miles per hour through the yellow dunes

the Red Dragon screams

floating through space

spinning on two wheels

my body screams

we are going to die

we are going to go down in the Red Dragon in El Centro, California

poet dies in a dune buggy flip

with LA-based photographer, really kind of amazing

Garrett Cornelison

Terry the Terror rips up and over the peak of a sand dune

our nose tips down to hell

and back up to heaven

I didn't see any of it

eyes shut

nails scraping into Garrett's hand and my seat

I open one eye

it's like a bad dream

the roller coaster to hell

all sorts of incomprehensible words come from my mouth
on the sound system we are all plugged into

I close my eyes

wish for it over

I see a flash of him swigging a Corona before we took off

his wife making a joke that he's half-blind

we're going to die

my body screams

we screech to a stop

I drop my clothes and walk naked along the line of a
yellow sand dune

the blue mountains and pink sky kissing the heavens

Terry and his wife sit below with the Red Dragon

as the camera clicks and life rolls on.

IT'S COLD MONTREAL

I lie in bed

at 12:41 PM

and listen to the rain

it drips

and falls gently into the world below

I hear the hum of voices

their feet falling

their red shoes

the dogs barking

it is a quiet world today

I don't wish to join them

today I wish to stay inside

just lie inside these white sheets

and be alone with the pitter putter

part of me feels I should go outside

and join the day

there are people with wet umbrellas in coffee shops

there is steam rising and falling from mugs of black
coffee beneath warm voices that fly above them

there are people running

wet and in the way

and if I am truly honest with you

I'm lying here because my heart is blue

last night I gave myself to a man who wasn't sure

and I wanted him to be sure

so I gave myself to him

and when I give my body away I feel as if I give away my power

even if that isn't true

or maybe it is

I'm not sure what right is right or left is left

I just wish to pull the covers over my head

I picked up my life and came here for a man who wasn't sure of me

my life is full and alive and I keep wasting it on men who don't have time

don't have time to smell more than my brown shoulder and soft skin

men who don't have time to stop and see the gentleness of my soul and the care in which I walk

for they are talking all night over a glass of red wine about themselves

and I listen

and wait for my turn

wait for his eyes to look away from himself and to me and to say, and you?

but that time doesn't come

and it's cold

It's cold, Montreal

and the rain is falling

and this is not my home

the tongue is not mine

the food is not mine

I do not connect to the connected, and I do not connect to the disconnected

I am lost in this world

I know my world

I know myself

but sometimes when I leave

and give myself away

I lose myself

I just wish for a man who is straight with me

I wish for a man who is kind with me

who is waiting outside with a black cup of coffee with the space to hear me

I wish for a man who looks at me with curiosity and sincerity

for he is looking for the point

and not a pit stop

I want a man who doesn't kiss me goodnight

I want a man who kisses me good morning

I feel closer these days, and I also feel further

for when you think you've found the point

and for them it was a pit stop

you question your compass

you question your intuition

when did you know?

why am I here?

I lie in bed

as my stomach grumbles—from discomfort or hunger

Why am I here on this rainy Tuesday in Montreal?
because you believe in love, dear one
the ghost above me sighs
but you must believe in one who believes in you
before they believe in love
love is not in the hands and heart of everyone
not love for you
love for this world—yes
but not for everyone

I curl into the white pillows
and turn my back to the people not paying attention
the ones out there who don't even know I exist
I'm tired from trying
I say
he sighs again
I know
you should not have come here
you should have waited for him to come to you
the one who believes in you will come to you
things like this make me want to close
I speak into the stillness of the white afternoon light
I know
you and every heart that beats
and we lie here
beat
beating
my blue heart and I.

AND A GODDESS JUST DOESN'T PUT UP WITH THAT SHIT

When a man's dick

has the attention span of the human population

who have the attention span of gerbils

eight seconds

it doesn't matter if he's married to a woman dripping in honey

a woman so sacred you'd love her if her legs were cut off

the second you stick your dick into another honey pot

you've pissed all over her sparkle

and a goddess just doesn't put up with that shit.

I SWEAR BECAUSE WOMEN ARE MEANT TO TASTE SWEET AND I TASTE OF SPICE

I swear because women are meant to be nice

and with my words I wish to start a fight with all that
must be broken open so we may be free

I swear for the cage you created for me the moment I was
born from the womb with a vagina is not the box I live in

I build my own box

it doesn't have the insistent cry of the children I won't
bring forth

or the yawn from my mouth at a desk with a job that
is killing a spirit I do not know is a spirit for I am so
disconnected from myself that I am lost

my box doesn't have the pension I won't ever spend
because I'm miserable with my existence and this will
manifest as dis-ease and pain and cancer and kill me
before I begin to live

I swear because the madness of people living in a world
that contains everything but the joy they seek drives me wild

I cannot contain my disdain for those who have quit living
while they still live

and when I swear

you listen

your ears stretch wide

for the world you live in is built for ladies

that curtsy and collect the children

bake cakes

and clean your beer bottles

as you fall asleep with a cigarette in your hands

I swear for I wish to break the chains from the throats of women who are afraid to speak

to disrupt

I wish to disrupt everything in your life that is parched dry of the authenticity of your soul

I wish to shake you into all that you are so that you may leave all that you pretend to be

I swear because we don't listen anymore

because good, fine, and okay

aren't even emotions

I want to hear your soul cry

your heart speak

I swear because our world still needs to be shouted at to listen sometimes

not all

but some

I swear because I like the way the energy in a room tenses as the words fall from my fiery tongue

I swear to get a rise from the parts of you that you do not know are sleeping.

I close my eyes

and see him there

the water is silver like heaven

the sky is white like God

black birds fly above him

like the orchestra

he floats

I paddle towards him and want to remember this moment
for the rest of my life

On my deathbed

I will close my eyes

and wish for this moment to visit me

there are only a few humans who make me feel so
connected

so alive.

–for Seth

You're a diamond
in a world full of other diamonds
who think they are pebbles.

Some women are storms
beautiful storms
to love.

I don't care if he is a wounded boy

anymore

I am not a daycare

for his self-realization

I am not his mother

here to cradle him

I am a woman

looking for a man

who has moved beyond his wounds

who does not hide from them

who has sat in the lava of his pain

and came out composed of stone

and I want to lay in his hands

knowing there is no earthquake that can shake him free.

I am not a pit stop
I am the point.

I show him all my cards

I am a woman

who doesn't know how to be anything but telling.

HE REACHES INSIDE MY UNDERWEAR

and his hand just stays there

strongly

firmly

softly

as his tongue dances in my mouth

my mouth could be a vagina kissing him feels so good

so strong

he played with the purple of my hard nipples for hours

making love with my breasts

teasing and tracing around them

before he dove into them like he was entering me for the
first time

and there his fingers are

in just the way they should be

with the strength and love that all women want to be
touched with

the pink of me moans

I am going to explode with the energy rushing up and
down my spine

he is inside of me

inside my mouth

inside the purple flesh of my nipples

inside the pinkness of my thighs

his fingers continue

and I continue to fall

and as I fall I wonder if any of the love I have ever made

has really been love

for none of them touched me with the tenderness of this

none of them touched my body as if it was the sacredness of the sun

I am beyond

I am gone

if I was only touched by those ten fingers and that tongue for the rest of my life, I would die happily alive

I wish for him to make love to every woman on this earth

and I also wish to bury him into my bosom and never let him go.

The plane shakes
my belly drops
oh God
please do not fall from the sky
please do not fall from the sky
I have so much living
so much time I need to be alive
do not take me yet
I beg of you

We burst through the grey of the clouds
and into the yellow and purple sky
I am not taking you yet, child
God yells down

It's enough to make me believe in a god at all.

I walk deliriously tired through the Montreal airport

I see a businessman

in a black suit

and a blue shirt

wearing a black eye mask

sitting on a red bench by the Uber pickup area

exit 6

he half-lifts his eye mask

squinting out at this fucking world

looking left and right

it's the best thing I've ever seen.

Finished? What is finished? We have just begun.

I have just became. I have felt this sand in my toes yet every morning it feels not the same.

I will never be finished with the sun burning in a red-hot ball as she sinks her teeth into the blue that hums on forever full of sea creatures as we stare, dazed and locked in awe as the sun does what she does every day. She is not finished; she is just breaking, taking a breath—for herself, for us, for the moon to stand tall and shine with the luster of a million stars cascading face-first into our hearts.

Finished? I have just begun to fall deeper in love with the people I've known for years—with the way she drags her feet and her things, tired, like a five-year-old, after surfing our brains out all morning.

I've cracked open layers of people I've seen and known yet never sat with. Shared moments where my heart cries, that's it!, as we bump across the blackness in a boat looking for hope, looking for faith, looking for something that lasts longer than lust.

This love story is just beginning (again).

MENSTRUATION CUPS ARE COOL

until they're leaking

and you're in an airplane washroom

trying not to sit on anything

or touch anything

hovering and squatting

with your fingers covered in blood

up your uterus

trying not to gush blood on anything

fishing around in there

and your hands probably aren't clean

fuck

the manual says to wash your fucking hands

I'm going to get an infection

I think

and then you're apologizing to God

and whatever sucker is waiting in line after you

as you wash the pink cup covered in blood

in the sink in the bathroom

and shove it back up there in all its glory

and then you have to shove paper towel into your
underwear

a homemade pad

because that motherfucker is leaking

and you're on a goddamn airplane

evolve or die they say

I think I choose to die using tampons

along with all the other stubborn women
who've been here.

The author retracts the point of this poem.
She is now pro-menstruation cups. Love your earth any way you can.

THE AMBULANCE SIREN SCREAMS

and screams

and screams

and screams

I take to the window

and see a row of cars in NYC not moving

I see the toes of a man through the back of the ambulance

on a white bed

a paramedic in a blue uniform beside him

he is someone's uncle

someone's dad

someone's brother

the cars, they do not move

the ambulance continues to scream

how long will his heart beat?

I almost open my window

hang my head out into the night and scream

move!

for the cars are still in his way

he may not live

there is a human life inside that ambulance

all of me wishes to cry

his heart

how long will his heart beat?

If I could turn every car honk
in New York City into a dollar bill
I'd be rich.

HE DID NOT KISS ME IN THE STINK AND SCREAM OF NYC

I sit in an all-white apartment
eating raspberries and blueberries
and it's the only thing that's sweet about this night
sometimes we have grand expectations
that he'll be there
with those sparkling eyes
that buckled our heart's knees
and those silver hairs in his curls
smiling
leaning against his car at JFK
but he wasn't
he forgot I was even coming in that day
and I took an Uber
with air conditioning too strong
and sat in silence for forty-five minutes

I thought that when I told him
I'm here
he'd jump in his car and race to see me
with the longing of a child on Christmas morning
for I am the greatest gift
but he didn't
he barely wrote me back

We did not drink big glasses of red wine by candlelight in
the basement of a smoky jazz bar in Brooklyn

he did not hold my hand and pull me back into him
and kiss me in the stink and scream of NYC
no one walked by and said
get a room
as our tongues finally tangled
under the black pollution and white moon

Instead, I turned off the lamp beside my bed
and held a pillow
listening to the air conditioner chug
with the heat of a red water bottle beside me

I did not wake to him calling
saying
darling let's have coffee
and then breakfast
and then life

I didn't hear from him all day
and when I did
he didn't rush to me
with the urgency of the dusk crickets as the sun expires at
first night
I walked home alone
and listened to the warmth of humans
and love
and wine
in white sneakers

carrying a bag of groceries

what a grand disguise

the great romances we give air

that disappoint us

before they even exist.

I'm too sweet

for this city

its people

with their black sleepless bags

their propped hats

I ooze like a sincere purple fig all over these streets.

People call me gullible
I call myself
sincere.

I sit in my apartment in Brooklyn

cuddling a hot water bottle

after struggling to insert a menstrual cup (but winning)

and it's 8:47 PM

and every few minutes I check my phone

because he surely will have written

but he hasn't

if he was the one

he would have been waiting with coffee before the
workshop began

kissing me on the forehead and wishing me good luck

he might have even been there

at the workshop

smiling at me

as I shine

in my big light

doing my dance

if he was the one

he would have been waiting for me

after the workshop

leaning against the stairwell

holding my tired body

picking up my bag

putting his arm around me

half-carrying me

because he knows I've given away my light for the day

and then we'd huddle over miso soup

and eat sushi

and I'd talk about how well it went

and how excited I am

and he wouldn't need anything

he wouldn't need me

all he would need is to be next to me

and when I realize I'd been talking about myself and my
work for twenty minutes

I'd get embarrassed and make a face

and he would grab my hands and laugh and smile

and ask me not to apologize

for he loves my stories

and when I am in my light

I go to text him

but then I stop

because if he was the one

I wouldn't need to think about whether I should text him

there wouldn't be any games

or any grey

it would be easy.

No rain that exists that could ever put out my sunshine—
for my spirit it roars, even when the heavens open—my
flames will meet you. It doesn't matter what I touch, for it
turns to wildfire. It doesn't matter how cold and barren or
how abundant the places are that I end up, for I have a well
of love inside me that is deep enough to feed us both—feed
us all. I have been practicing this for a long, long time.

You may bring your heavens, your thunder, your lightning,
your flood—no rain exists that could ever put out my sparkle.

I ache

alone

I ache alone in this sea of red hearts that beat

I ache alone

in a room full of people laughing

I ache alone

in hugs where our hearts don't touch

I ache alone in a warmth that is temporary

and misleading

for it is the warmth that begins

and once you feel safe and like you can uncurl your soul

unguarded and accepted

it drops you

I ache here amongst the stars

and the crickets

and the yellow flowers

for I do not know where I belong.

YOU MUST BELONG SO DEEPLY TO YOURSELF THAT A ROOM FULL OF TURNED BACKS DOESN'T MAKE YOU TURN YOUR BACK ON YOUR LIGHT

The moments where we feel alone
in a room full of people
warm and laughing
are the reason we cling to our solitude
our independence
they are why we climb the tree
into the sky
and throw away the key to our hearts

I gave it to them
we tell God
I gave it all to them and they didn't want it
they didn't want me

And God will listen
as we cry
as we swear we have no place in this world
except within ourselves
and that we will now live alone
and never let anyone close enough to not let us in
not save a seat for us
not ask us who we are
and why we laugh
and love

and live

and cry

For that is God's job

to listen to you when you have forgotten your light

and let you believe that you have no light

for long enough that you have empathy for the others that
struggle to be here

that struggle to find their place in a room

in a job

in this world

in love

You feel alone now

God sighs and then continues

because you are held by the hands of a thousand suns

you are alone now

so you may arrive even deeper into your belonging

for just because we do not always connect

and others do not connect

it doesn't mean that we don't deserve the seat

or the success

or the love

it doesn't mean that they are more than

or we are less than

But it is!

you cry

they didn't like me!

not like her

not like him

they ran

and they did not care if I followed

and that broke my spirit into a thousand pieces

so deeply that I wanted to lock myself into a room and cry
until my sadness became a river that washed away anyone
close enough to hurt me

And then God would lift his face in a sort of you're right
and you get it half-frown

for he sees a world who doesn't feel

who doesn't see the light in the sadness

and the sadness in the light

And after he has listened

and you are done crying

and speaking

and hurting

he will kneel

and look you in the eyes

with a deep enough look that your light starts to burn in
your toes and climb

climb to your heart

to your spine

You are the light

God says

and they are the light

and you will always belong to one another

but you must first belong to yourself

belong so deeply to yourself that a room full of turned
backs

doesn't make you turn your back on your light

My dear one

you are never alone

it's impossible

those backs are a mirror to the back you turn on your light

All there is

is light

all you are

is light.

BEAUTY IS NOT ALWAYS THE BEST
MESSENGER FOR WISDOM

I imagine that your work is hard

she says

as we hold mint tea

over a field of yellow grass

under blankets in the wild of Quebec

for you are sincere

she continues

in a world that isn't honest

and you are also beautiful

and young

with eyes that sparkle

and beauty is not always the best messenger for wisdom

And a part of me exhales so deeply that I become the wind

for I've been crucified from the day I shot from the womb

and sometimes I wish to rip my face in half

so that the world could take it

take what I am here to give

what I have to say

what I have to share

for it is important

and they cannot bear the message

for it comes from a woman as old as their daughter

and wisdom only comes with age

yes, wisdom only comes with age

how could wisdom come from anything other than our age?

except when it doesn't.

I wish to be the one

to walk up to him

intentionally and slowly

as he lights the orange of a cigarette in the night rain

to walk with eyes that sparkle like sunflowers with
midnight blue

into him

to take up the space

to begin the beginnings

but I look at him

in the rain

in the night

and I walk away.

MY KNEES SHAKE
more often than I stand tall
my shoulders concave
more than my shoulders are square
I demand that women walk tall
because in them
I find my spine.

PAPARAZZI

hunt for secrets

waiting in the bushes

to catch and expose moments

moments that make someone the bad guy

I write a book

and in it

tell you

that I fucked a man

who wasn't mine

Maybe that makes me mad

maybe it means you can finally breathe.

We are always fighting our demons

in everyone else

but ourselves.

Do I belong here?
I call to the crickets
as they rub the yellow and brown of their wings

Do I belong here?
I howl at the white of the husky's face
grey seeping over a face of wisdom

Do I belong here?
I peer into the green of the lake
the water hurts my eyes
the fish peer up at me
you don't have gills
they bubble

I go to the two-leggeds
but my voice is quiet
it doesn't quite open
and my heart it aches
blue in my chest.

I'M GETTING SO GOOD AT BEING HATED

I'm feeling a little numb now

in a beautiful way

their words are there

like I know they will be

but the words don't sink their teeth as deeply as they used
to

it doesn't sting the same

I know what they are going to say before they even say it

being hated is just part of the work that I'm doing

like when you drive

it's assumed that someone's going to be an asshole

riding your ass

cutting you off

being a writer online means the ones who don't have
spines are given a space to let their rage seep

but it doesn't touch me the same

and now I'm grateful that they're just feeling

feeling anything at all.

And then I drink champagne

and eat oysters

alone at sunset

on Halloween

avoiding the kids I don't have candy for

and think about all the sex I feel like having with all the
men I shouldn't want tonight

I think about throwing the one with the British accent
across a wall

and fucking him till the sun comes out

and the one with the ripped jeans

that I feel a heat in between my legs when he's near

I want to bite his bottom lip so hard it bleeds

feel his rough calloused fingers

upon my white breasts and purple nipples as he fights
with the zipper on my jeans.

I WANT HIM LIKE I WANT TO FEEL MY BARE FEET RUN

I find his cigarette in my alpaca rug

I feel his cum dried on the corner of my white couch

I taste him in the morning on my tongue

I smell him on my skin

I want him like I want to feel my bare feet run.

ONCE YOU SEE THE WRITING ON THE WALL

And it happens

quite quietly

really

after all the yelling

and the door slamming

and the pizza boxes being thrown

and the morning-after knock on the door

and coffee

and eggs

and sweetness

it just takes him sitting under the moon

exclaiming

right now he can't do it

even if he wanted to

and that he goes in and out

in all love

and then something inside me releases

and it's not fighting or sad

it just releases

and I can look at him

from afar

and smile

and have love

but not be tormented inside

for the writing is written on the wall

and once you see it

you can't help but find a new wall.

Here I go again
falling in love
with an idea
of a man

If he isn't the man
it will be nice
to have loved love
again.

WHOEVER SAID ONE PERSON CAN'T CHANGE THE WORLD DIDN'T KNOW A FUCKING THING

We are all rushing

under the hot afternoon sun

going to our jobs

our lovers

grocery stores

gas stations

busy

busy

rushing

suddenly the light turns orange

and we all slam on the brakes

hard

a small woman

hunched over in her eighties

takes the crosswalk

slowly

taking up the space

pausing us humans

our busy lives

whoever said one person can't change the world

didn't know a fucking thing.

I WILL EAT YOU ALIVE

He writes me

to come

and part of me loves the flow

the unguided guide

the idea of him here

for a day

or a week

drinking coffee out of those coffee cups

and then part of me wants to grab his balls

with one hand

so tight he can't breathe

and force my other hand inside his chest cavity and hold
his red glistening bloody heart

and say

boy

don't play with me

don't walk into the waters of my life

carelessly

intentionless

I will eat you alive.

THERE SHOULD BE YELLING STATIONS IN OUR WORLD

I am glad when humans yell

when they don't yell

it turns into cancer

or liver disease

there should be yelling stations in our world

like a smoking booth in an airport

except you just go in and rage

safely

privately

and then you can carry on empty with your day.

For those of us who aren't wounded

the wounded ones can lash out

and they don't hurt us

for we know they are living through the gaping

seeping

holes in their hearts.

I WANT A MAN TO CLIMB UP MY SOUL

one arm lifting him

after the other

and drink my nectar

like the honey I am

there has been too much sex

and not enough soul ripples

too much touching

just to enter

too many orgasms

that lack the synchronicity I dream of

too many nights where I have woken next to a tossed bed
and a blond head

put my heart's ear to the body next to me

and not felt the beat of intimacy

there is sex

and there is making love

and I'm only signing up for making love from here on out

I want the lovers to fall to my knees like flies stuck in
honey

and carve the insides of my legs

until my body turns the ground into an earthquake

and then enter me with not only the purple of my nipples

the mountains of my breasts

but the blue and grey and green speckles of my eyes

as we fall apart together.

HE'S GOING TO BE A QUIET MAN

and maybe he won't be quiet

but it

will be quiet

the it

when he walks through the door

with no dance

no fuss

no flight

it will be quiet when we choose that we are who we wish
to choose

it will be quiet at night

and in the mornings

because there won't be this tremendous push and pull

this game

I'm not signing up for fight-or-flight love anymore

I'm going to sit here and wait for a quiet love to walk
straight in my door

straight in

not through the back

or the side

or the window

I'm going to see him coming

in the warmth of his hands

the vulnerability of his heart

the sturdiness of his spirit

he's going to walk straight through that door

and I'm just going to look up and smile

because I've already chosen him

and I knew he was coming

right for me.

My love, I don't want to leave the woods.

Will you come find me and we just stay?

The waves are here every day, the water is white and gold.
The seaweed is red. It is quiet. It is cozy here with the
hemlocks and the spruce trees.

I crave this more than I knew. I resent all that calls to me
other than the call of the eagles as they circle overhead.

I am at home here, in between the trunks of the big
spruce trees—washing my bowl in the cold ocean water.
This is the only sink I need.

I'll shower in the waterfall and stay, oh—please just let me
stay.

I'll gladly give it all away to stay.

I wish for a dozen fireflies and hummingbirds to dip and sing honey into your ears as you fall asleep tonight. I wish for the stars to dance for you—just for you—and for the moon to make a private trip to your window to read you a story that is full of humans that are kind, and love, lots of love. I wish your sheets to hold your body so sweetly that it lets go of everything today that didn't feel like a bath after a cold walk in the purple mountains. I hope that you feel the love and the weight of a million puppies as you lie down in bed tonight—that you feel their sweet weight on your side. I hope that you fall asleep in a bed full of petals of all the grandest flowers—sunflowers and red roses and pink roses. I hope that your pillow hugs you a little when you get in, as if to say, "Oh! you're here, I've waited all day for you."

And if none of that happens, I just wanted to tell you I am sure happy you are alive.

I THINK THAT WHEN HE FINALLY SHOWS UP

I'm going to have to cry

I'm going to need to cry to let go of not trusting men

I'm going to need to cry to let go of not needing men

I'm going to need to cry to let go of my belief that I'll be let down by men

I'm going to need to grieve twenty-nine years of the wrong men

to make space for him

and I want to say I can do it without him

I am

I have

but I think that when my heart finally feels safe

not just alone

but in the hands of another

and it truly feels and believes that it is safe

that it's going to need to collapse

It's going to need to receive twenty-nine years of presence I haven't had

it's going to need to receive twenty-nine years of understanding and compassion for how much I feel and how much of a woman I am

it's going to need to receive a lifetime making up for a lifetime of men who did not have large enough hands to hold me

It is going to take a tall, strong, and soft man to hold the heart and woman that I am

for once he is here
I am going to cry until my tears become rivers
and lakes
and then the ocean
and I am going to need him to keep his feet
planted firmly on land

In fact, I might need him to be the earth
for a decade
and just let me swim in the ocean that I am
until it's safe for me to surface fully onto dry land.

IT SURE IS EXHAUSTING BEING THE SPARKLE

especially when you can't admit to people

exasperated that you are the sparkle

the man working in the deli at the grocery store

who asks to have coffee because you feel so good

the gentleman working the fruits

who chases you down and asks for a coffee

I don't want to go for a coffee

you just like my sparkle

and I don't like you

I feel safe with you

I can talk to you

I collect numbers of men and women of every age

they want to connect

and our connection is genuine

it's just a connection I genuinely want for five minutes

not a connection I want to nurture and love

no

that's not with you

you just like my sparkle

and some days I wish to go to the grocery store

or a shop

without having a forty-minute conversation with a man
chasing me down to be in his life

I'd like to be horridly ugly

and dull

and not sparkly

or I'd like to know my sparkle

and my beauty

and be downright wicked

use it

but I'm none of those things

oh—brother

I'm sparkly

and I'm kind

and I don't know how to look them in the eye and say

I won't give it to you

past these five minutes

past these ten seconds

I only wish to sparkle with you when it is in the path

in flow

you cannot trap my light

I am not like some firefly you may keep in your pocket

let me go.

He shows up
with hands that have no fingers
and expects me to wish him to hold me

I look at his hands
his empty promises
and walk away

The man who holds me
will need eight arms
and forty fingers
and sometimes to borrow the hands of God to encompass
the woman that I am.

I have a degree
in crucifying
men.

You've fucked yourself to me?

good

I've fucked myself to you, too.

CUM ON THE COUCH

pillows on the floor

walking around at 11 AM wondering where my other
brown shoe is

almost give up after five minutes

to find it shoved inside the couch

along with my tights

that you ripped off

with my black bodysuit

as your tongue found my lips

and shook my body awake

To think I settled for anything short of you

to think this may only happen once

I don't think I can afford not to make love to you

again

and again

and again

I want to feel your bottom lip

and your hands

and your teeth on my nipples

I want to lie sideways

and beside you

and love you while we play

Can I love you now?

there's been plenty of play

now I want to fumble with our shirts, hurriedly as we
rush to undress.

It was so good
I almost didn't feel bad about it
until I felt bad about it.

They really have to treat you with the sacredness that you are

from the moment they meet you

or they're fucked

a woman never forgets the moment you piss on her sparkle.

WHEN YOU FIND YOUR POWER

It is a beautiful thing
to acquaint yourself with your power
to turn a corner one day
to be faced with the light of a thousand suns
to be blinded by all that you are
your spine feels taller
your voice deeper
your eyes clearer

Yes
then
they can hit you
but it doesn't knock the air out of you quite the same
and they can love you
but it doesn't seep into the holes in your insecurity you
once had
momentarily floating you above the surface
instead it floats by gently
because you now understand that you were always above
surface
breathing air

When you find your power
the only one who can cut you
and shatter you
or make you grow taller
is you

When you find your power

your legs realize that they've been holding you

all along

and how weak the temporary hands that supported you
really are in comparison

When you find your power

you will no longer be gasping for oxygen from the hands
of others

you will be walking upon water like God.

Do not look to me
to fill your seeping holes
I am not the ocean
I am her mighty sister.

Easy with your fists
they are the size of God's thumbs.

My dharma is a beast
it could keep me up all night
and all day
for when we find what we love
we let it burn until we have no fingers left.

My favourite part
was watching him
watching her
sing.

THERE IS A WICKED WOMAN

who lives in my heart

she has food in her teeth

and her underwear aren't fresh

and when she sees the muck that men sometimes are

she wants to lean back

chewing on a toothpick

and crucify their souls with a cruelty the rest of me doesn't
dare understand

only observes

Tonight she almost took your heart apart with a steak
knife

while the rest of me smiled.

This week there is a thunderstorm

and I am sitting naked

in a puddle

holding a green banana leaf over my head

there is no mercy from this world

so I lay in the bottom of the shower and let the hot water
beat and beat upon me until I feel lighter.

Inside I am a soul
screaming and kicking around
like all of you.

YOU INSPIRE THEM BECAUSE YOU ARE THE
ONLY ONE WHO MOVES YOUR OWN LIPS

They ask me how I do it
and I tell them
after a while it gets less hard

Except for the days
the gunfire is so loud it seeps into my heart
and I feel them yelling and screaming
pounding on my back
and it's so loud
that I question myself
God, I hate that I question myself
I know I am the only one who should question myself

But when it gets this loud
I do
and then I am a child
sitting on the floor
unsure of what I have said wrong
if I am the monster they say I am
or whether I am right
and I am not
and what is right?
right
wrong
we all have the purple claws of monsters inside of us

and today they tear at me

and inside I am a ship in stormy waters

trying to find the ground

where is the ground?

where are my feet?

who am I?

am I that?

did I harm?

should I remove what I wrote?

should I spend ten hours researching and informing
myself?

No!

part of me rages

you are not here to be a puppet to speak to that which
others find important

you are here to move your very own arms and legs

to walk

and sit

and dance

as you please

you are here to speak to only that which calls your soul

and you are not to be shamed

or made guilty

all of the humans of this world have voices to speak

let them speak for themselves if they wish something
addressed

to use your voice to what they ask

is the opposite of what you live

it's to conform

it's to become that which you detest

you inspire them because you are the only one who moves
your own lips

when we let others move our arms with their strings

we have given away our power

our sacred duty and right to be

Yes, but they say I have a duty

because there are so many eyes

the eyes

oh, the eyes

they burn

like a million stars

like the flame in the heat of the night

do I have a duty?

are they right?

should I watch my tongue as it moves now?

I have never watched my tongue

I don't want to watch my tongue

I want it to roll

like pink flesh

around and around

as I become more of that which I am and that which I am
not

I want my tongue to speak too quick

and too slow

and to only learn by knowing when I am abandoning
myself and when I am too quick

I have a temper that boils

she rages inside

the rebel in me wants to break the fingers pointing at me

point at you!

this is your pain

that you paint me with

this is your fear

your unhappiness

your shit that you smear on my face

And the child inside of me cries

for she does not feel understood

she feels demonized

she feels judged

she feels their claws ripping through the flesh of her heart
and she howls

don't they understand?

she whimpers

I am not that!

I am this!

I am light!

I am love!

make them understand!

she is on her knees now
with snot on her face
make them understand that I am not that!

And I sit solemnly
in an airport lounge massage chair
tears falling
falling
falling
they drip drop on the back of my hand
and my soul drains

I do not have the answer

But in these moments
and on these days
I nearly go mad
I wish to run from their voices and my work
deep into the forest
and sit beside the frogs
and count their croaks
I wish to peer at the moon
with a vulnerable heart
and be held by the salt of the ocean

In these moments, it isn't clear
and I am not wise
I am a child in a gunfight

and I am bleeding

angry

wounded

In these moments

I forget who I am

and become who you believe I am

and I must grieve those who don't understand and leave

I must love the parts of me that shrivel in pain

I must hold myself as tightly as I can and remember the
sun will always shine again

and even deeper than that

I must remember that I am the sun

and the claws are also the sun

and that there is no fight.

What was that?
I was too busy
dismantling your shoulds
and listening to the cry of my own spirit
instead.

FOR THE WOMEN WHO FORGET THEIR LEGS

I don't approve

of these men

that are like lions

who live in their large caves

in LA

Hollywood

Venice Beach

with houses with six bedrooms

and all the women who are also lions but still believe they
are mice

living downstairs

thank you

holy saint

thank you

king

he is not a king

you are a queen

giving your power away

when he never asked

to live in the dungeon

degrading yourself to a room on the bottom floor

that you don't pay for

so you never challenge yourself to stand

to look down and realize your legs are just as sturdy as his

that your muscles ripple

screaming at you to stand

that your feet are powerful

like a puma's

and they are ready to grip the earth of everything you seek

and run

throwing this man

preying on the weak

preying on those that think they need him

when they only need themselves

into the trenches of who they were when they had not yet
touched the center of their own power

This is why

I will not come to LA

and stay in a room of a rich and famous

if he is housing hordes of women who foolishly believe
that he is their knees

And to the men

who need to be needed

by these hordes of helpless women

damsels

flies

now I am speaking to you

quit needing to be needed

and hear the cry that you need to need yourself.

Speak for us!

they yell

speak for us!

No!

I bellow down

I am here because I only speak the thunder in my belly

do you not have a tongue?

and lips?

like I?

did God not give you the exact same tools as I?

do not ask me to be your tongue.

If you march into my home

on a Saturday

while I am sitting in my pajamas

yawning and just waking up

and demand that I drink my coffee

with cream

and two sugars

because you believe that is how I should drink it

I will throw hot brown liquid

that scalds your eyeballs

and whisper in your ear

while you scream

no, I take it black.

Some days they tenderly kiss my feet
worshipping the bottoms of my toes who hold me
and the next
they take steel nails
and hammers the size of Jupiter
and nail me to the cross of everything they believe I am
and everything I am
and am not.

MY THUNDER KEEPS ME SANE

What's it like?

sharing slabs of your heart for a living?

I look up

with eyes of ocean blue

it's like thunder

I reply

thunder so loud that some days it could very well beat out
of my chest

thunder of millions of fists and voices drinking and
spitting up the most vulnerable crevices of my soul

thunder full of rain

so loud and so heavy

that it breaks the roof in

and you're left sitting in a puddle

fingers stabbing away at all you have left

for when you are a writer

the thunder in your soul

is always louder than the thunder in the streets

and if we stopped writing

we would break open and apart

my thunder keeps me sane

your thunder drives me mad.

Sometimes
in a forest fire
the wisest thing we can do
is be still.

Of course I see a therapist

it's my pen

she saves me every time.

Some days
I walk tall
and some days
their words break my spine.

I AM WITHIN THE WILDEST WAR
inside of myself
I want to write down every blink of my father's brown eyes
every stroke of his brown
salt-and-peppered grey beard

I want to write the white of his cigarette papers
the marijuana he hides secretly in his ring

I want to write the red tile
the yellow tile
the blue tile
dancing in his garden
with the large heart rock

I want to write the smell of his house
made entirely of natural elements
from his hands
of his bed
full of thyme
of his ritual area—where he does Osho dances and yoga
and shakes himself wildly awake

I want to write of the way his clothes fall on nails beside
the fireplace
wrinkled and loved

I want to write of the green pears he brings me in a brown
plastic bag

how he drives deep into the mountains

to gather fresh water from a spout

in large plastic bottles

because he doesn't believe in the well water from below
the ground

I want to write of the way he lights up when he is excited
by something

how he laughs and says I go crazy for the figs!

I lose myself for the figs!

and the colours—oh, the colours!

I want to write of the yellow plastic bags that he tied in the
mountains

so I could find his house

that he calls the roads earth streets

and tells me

if you get lost

just shout

and I will come find you

I want to write of his orange shirt

with frayed sides

his style is so beautiful

and feminine

many men think that I am gay, he says

cigarette between his lips

but I know from the man above the white house in the
mountains I am renting

that—your father

your father was wildly handsome, you know?

he's been with hundreds of women

I was jealous of him

I wish to write the way his cheeks move when he eats

as he has no teeth

and how he is handsome still

I wish to write of the sparkle in his eyes as he shows me
the things he makes with stones

sinks

stairs

fountains

of his excitement as he throws water upon the dusty
stones

and they shine red or lustrous black

how he exclaims

look! look!

how he believes these are the real riches

I wish to write the pure soul of him

one that many here wouldn't understand

for Tertsa is small

and he exists with the simplicity and richness in his mind
that many have not touched

and will not touch

And some of the people laugh at him, for his thoughts are
grand and larger than the world some people live within

I wish for him not to be mocked

but celebrated as I celebrate his thoughts

some people will never understand

I forgive them

but wish for people to see his light

as it is great

there is nothing small about his presence

I wish to write you and tell you of the time we walked
through the streets of Heraklion

his small brown arm with an orange bracelet draped upon
mine

of how proud this made me

to be walking arm in arm with my father

My father I found

Of how he bought me brown leather sandals

and a silver ring

of how I could have bought these for myself, but I said yes

and received

I wish to tell you that each time he arrives at my white
house in the mountains he brings gifts

small jars of coconut oil

a Robert Munsch book that my mother gave him twenty-
eight years ago

worn and eaten by life yet still attached

a small piece of peppermint

which he wisped underneath my nose

before handing me a leaf to eat

telling me every morning he drinks a warm cup of water

and chews a fresh peppermint leaf

he brings a piece of a plant that in Greek is called Louisa

my mother's name

and we walked

arm and arm to the small village

and I had my father in one hand

and my mother in the other

and how wild that is

your mother used to call me tatziki

in India

he says laughing

I wish to write you and tell you of how he always chooses
a tiny espresso cup

and how wonderful he looks

with his wild hair

and sun hat

in brightly coloured orange or pink clothing

drinking from a tiny delicate cup

as he reads me Greek poetry

that I pretend to understand while admiring the way his
hands dance when he speaks

admiring the way he's trying

he is trying

I wish to write you to tell you of the food he makes

fresh vegetables from his garden

of how his face lights up when he tastes the food he has made

of the pooaaa-pooaaa-pooaaa

noise that you will only understand after being in Greece

and hearing it escape from his mouth in appreciation for the simple yet extraordinary food he cooks

and how he brought two containers

and looked at me and said

I cooked two dishes—because, well, you are always very hungry

after watching me devour a large chicken souvlaki at lunch

and I laughed

as he may not know that I stress about food

yet I do

and he is right

I wish to write you and tell you of his small car

his tiny hippie car

the new white one

the sister of the blue one that died

it has feathers and necklaces hanging from the mirror

delightful things

gentle things

the doors don't lock

the seats are dead and he has put pillows and blankets

upon them

and sometimes it hurts my back after long drives

but it does the job

one day soon I will leave this car

he says

I will go and live in the caves

maybe when I am 70

(which is in 9 years)

and live up there alone

be in the natural

I wish to die under a tree

and before I die I will make a clear wish that I want my soul to live the next life on a different planet

if there is a different planet

I am done with this planet

and how I sit

wide-eyed in love with the peculiar and wonderful man he is

yet at the same time sit in fear that only after finding him he will retreat into a cave and I will lose him again

I wish to tell you of how the people stare at him

in the gyros shop

in Heraklion

this one young man never stopped staring

I'm not sure if it was him

or me with him

we are probably quite a sight

tall

lanky

skinny

tanned like olives

my father with wild hair and a large beard like he is
maybe Indian

like a guru or a yogi

round blue glasses like Tommy Chong

I wonder if they know I am his daughter

some people have thought I am his girlfriend

the age is so great now with couples

I guess this is normal

yet with the same ears and body and face in many ways

I wonder if they even look

I wish to write you the sounds of Crete

the roaring from these crickets that are not crickets

that live on the trees

with large wings

they yell louder than anything I have ever heard

it is overwhelming at dusk and dawn when I walk in the
dried river

through dusty roads with yellow dead grass weeping at my
tired feet

as I make the journey again and again

back to that which I fear and want most

I wish to tell you of the part of me that so badly wants to
run

the part of me that is wounded so deeply by my father's
choice not to raise me

not to see the photograph of me as a child and the letter
from my mother when I was one

and write back

to know

to be

Yes

this part of me has its heels planted deeply and is terrified
to be here

even though I am here

this part of me is angry and spiteful and says

for what?

why?

he didn't come

why?

Yet I am here

sitting at the table

underneath a large cedar tree

eating the brown buds of the cedar tree

sitting under the moon

by candlelight

as my father hates lights

hates electricity

hates computers

hates cellphones

hates the advancement our world has claimed

holding him adoringly in my eyes

Yet I am here

in his small white car

with eyes full of blue salty tears

speaking the anger and hurt and fears in my heart

Yet I am here

in his village of 60 people

with two restaurants

and one hotel

swimming in the sea that is me

eating gallons of olive oil

and discovering new parts inside of me

Yet I am here

in a small taverna

pulling forth that inside of me which may save me

be a salvation from the suffering I have endured

in this gap in my childhood

two amazing loving mothers

yet I always wanted to know

of course

why would we not want to know where we came from?

And he is here
I will get this phone
he says
with this video
(FaceTime)
and I will try this time
this time
it is different
I feel strong
undeniably
you are a part of me
and you deserve to know me
and I am also curious about you
I want to see
for us to go together

And I hear it
in the way his hand holds mine
and assures me
that I don't need to buy the phone
that he will

And I hear it in the woman in the restaurant in Myrtos
who when I say I am visiting
her eyes bug
and she says
only 8 days?

and he replies

yes

but she will make many more trips

And I struggle with whether I can forgive

with whether he deserves my forgiveness after choosing
not to be in my life for 21 years

yet my mentor gently reminds me

forgiveness isn't about him

it is about you

and healing yourself

And yet I want to forgive him

and not have such a weight in my chest when people ask
me

what of your father

and not to reply

he lives in Greece

but we have only met once

I want to be rid of this story

and simply to reply

yes, he lives in Greece

I wish to write all these things

and I wish to write nothing

for I want to be here in all that there is

and all that I am.

OH GREAT SPIRIT

Oh wild eyes

Oh wide heart

Oh great spirit

may you drink the yellow grass that is thirsting on the sides of the Cretan highways

may you put the blue of the never-ending sea inside the pocket of your soul for forever keeping

may you trap the sound of crickets calling at the world to slow down

even if we may never listen

I am listening

may we thank the mountain water that collects at our mouths to drink

the green pears that hang welcoming from the trees

pluck me; drink my juice

nourish your body

Oh great life

I am here within each side of your red heart that beats without us asking

that puts us to sleep with stars each night

and wakes us with the gift of a thousand suns

Who am I to be so lucky to wake up each day and live?

blessed is today for my eyes remain wide to see all that you are to me.

I CHOOSE MY CRAFT

A van full of children

he says

so many they can't fit in the vehicle

my eyes bug

how shall I write with children screaming and crying and
pulling and hungry and playing?

this man is a dream

but this may be my demise

how can I heed the craft and bear children?

I choose my craft.

I KNOW YOU BELIEVE THAT MY FEET ARE THE ONLY FEET THAT CAN WALK THIS WALK FOR US

While you are yelling
that I should be your hero
I am floating in the ocean
beside a man in his seventies
watching pelicans glide across the crest of waves like God

I am too busy filling my shoes with the feet I own
to fill the shoes you have built for me

I am busy
over here
watching the orange of garibaldi fishes
and the green seaweed swaying below

I am busy
over here
being everything I am
and nothing that you can ever understand

What is wrong with your feet?
can they not fill the shoes you built for me?
are they perhaps for you anyway?

I know you believe that they are my shoes to walk in
I know you believe that my feet are the only feet that can
walk this walk for us

and it's flattering
and in moments I hate you for that
and in others I love you for it
I love that you carved those shoes with your eyes on me
that you carefully made each side just perfect for my toes
intentionally and impactfully

Her light is so bright
she should wear these shoes
you said
she will carve the earth
she will walk this fight
yes
she is already being seen
she will see this
this is her duty
her walkabout
she will see

But, I am busy
over here
waiting for you
to be your own hero

I am busy over here
waiting for you to see your own light
and stand up to be seen

Those shoes never have been
and never will be for me

They are yours
and you tricked yourself
and almost me
into wearing them

I am busy
making my own shoes
that I intend to wear
and run in
until the soles of them are spent

And then I must sit still
and politely say no
to the rest of the shoes you have made for me

And decide where I will step next.

You are allowed to forget who I am
but I am not allowed to forget.

THE ANSWER TO THE WHY OF LIFE

is the feeling of the air

as it seeps softly between your fingers

as they hang from the open window of a white car with seats that are dead

as the wind flows and breathes between all that we are and all that we may become

if you must seek further

you are a fool for the hunt

this

my darling

is it.

WHO SURVIVES, SURVIVES

He carries a white plate

full of blond spaghetti

with a little meat and tomato sauce

down the stairs

there's a whole family of them now!

he remarks

blue striped pants

wild hair

he calls them and then scrapes the spaghetti onto a dish

the two white and grey cats run over

one child cat runs over

there's another one somewhere, he says

looking around

well!

he throws his hands up

and his wild hair looks like that of a scientist who's been
electrocuted

while inventing something

I just feed them

who survives, survives

and he walks up the stairs.

ALL FINISHED, BOSS?

he says

I always tell him he's the boss

but today I am not my usual witty self

he comes behind the counter

where I sit with a black coffee

and breakfast being hovered over by big black flies

grabs a small plastic bag for something

where is your friend?

the man?

your boyfriend

he is gone

just three days?

he looks concerned

he's a new boyfriend, I smile back

he makes a face

I hope you have another guest soon

I smile softly

perhaps he thinks I'm lonely

perhaps I am

and then he leaves

see you Saturday, boss.

I WOKE UP THIS MORNING

and when I saw your name
my heart didn't skip the same

I woke up this morning
and there wasn't a sparkle
or a luster in my eyes for you

I woke up this morning
and can no longer see a big van
overflowing with the kids you wished with me

I woke up this morning
and can no longer feel the sea of Spain
on my skin

I woke up this morning
and can no longer see the white sailboat
the grey sweater you would wear
the hand of yours I would hold
as the sun sank its teeth into the ocean

I woke up this morning
and can no longer feel Stockholm in summer
I don't know what my boots would feel like
walking across the pavement to greet you

I woke up this morning
and can no longer see you driving down to California

beside me

our blond hair kissing the sun through the roof of my jeep

I woke up this morning

and can no longer hear your feet walking across the
wooden floor of my home in Cardiff

as you wake to fetch tea

I woke up this morning and my soul is already rinsing
itself of you.

I am beside myself

with the feelings of hundreds of people I do not know

it is stuck to me

like superglue

I pull at their anger

I yank at their sadness

I struggle with their insecurity

I kick at their blame

I rip at their disdain

I lean into their love

and then realize

I don't want it either

for it is the same.

I'd like to write a book about how to write non-fiction for
a living

and not go mad

but the truth is

to write non-fiction for a living

you must be mad.

You say you'll never be
the other woman
until you are.

Apparently the devil drinks gluten-free hibiscus
kombucha beer

after fucking men who aren't hers

and calls it a night.

I stare the brown bottle in the face

knowing I should run

pretend I'm being dragged by the ear

but I stare at it

like the feeling you have when you're both finally naked

and you should put a condom on

but you just want to feel him

just feel the tip of him on your lips for a moment

have him feel your wetness

the energy surging in your body

asking him to take you

come in

that's what buying a beer means

on a day where you know you're going straight to the dark
side of hell.

We are all capable of hellish things
and last night I tasted them
on the lips of a man
that wasn't mine.

I ALWAYS SAID I WOULD NEVER BE THE OTHER WOMAN

yet I was

and I am

how do I walk through this world

knowing in a moment of lust

and tequila

and a dive bar where the carpets smell like skanky piss

that I took his whole body

his whole mouth

and devoured him?

while she lay in her bed at night

waiting with their dogs

in their sheets

with their toothbrushes

and I fucked him

on my white couch

with my shoes on

and the lights on

and the blinds open

and I didn't care

because it felt right

I wonder if at the gates of hell

it felt right

will serve as an alibi?

I am not afraid to be your villain
I am not afraid to show you
the darkness
you have inside of yourself.

I can tell a lot about someone's laugh
I can feel their joy
their purity
their madness clap off the walls
the manic in them drumming its fingers
my whole spirit feels people's laughs
and it either leans back
or propels me deeper into them.

We lock eyes and lightning runs through my entire body

as he pours me tea he says

you do not have eyes

you have galaxies.

THAT SILENCE YOU'VE BEEN AFRAID TO HEAR IS ACTUALLY THE MOST BEAUTIFUL MUSIC YOU'VE EVER LAID EARS ON

Brown bottles

empty bottles

full bottles

yellow labels

they go for the bottles like some lungs ask for air

they drown in these bottles

white hands reaching

reaching into the back of a fridge for a bottle

bottles of void

bottles of avoidance

bottles of fear

bottles of protection

bottles of self-loathing

bottles of boredom

bottles of a lack of curiosity and desire for the sparkle and gleam in each moment

each other's eyes

bottles of bottles of emptiness

and you put them inside of you

and they all fit

they all fit until they don't fit anymore

until you wake up

one day

so empty in your chest

and realize you've been poisoning yourself your entire life

and that the silence you've been afraid to hear

well, that silence is actually the most beautiful music
you've ever laid ears on.

BALI

Crusted in salt

pull over in a warung that we don't know

that is just there

on the way

flies hovering over yellow chicken

drenched in red chili flakes

greens

rice

a mystery curry

potatoes

corn fritters

the food piles and piles

I feed the dog chunks of chicken

held a puppy the other day

four weeks old

it looked up at me with small black beady eyes

in awe

what a crime to be born a dog in Bali

it is not easy here

I leave my leftovers by the trashcan every night

but it isn't enough

I pay $7 for two heaping plates of food

smile with my eyes at the women behind the counter

say goodbye to the dog

wagging its tail for today it cut a break

flashes of oysters crusting the reef

water falls as if it's raining

men and women fall from the cliffs below throwing their
surfboards at the last second

I wonder how often their boards get in the way of it

and then the sets come

and you must paddle right there

beside that rock

and it takes you

gently and strongly

all the way left

except when it holds you under something strong

and you just pray like hell the reef lets you pass go and
collect $200

limbs spent

watching a man with the style of a snake

droop gracefully down the line

body hovered over himself

hands flowing

the fishermen throw their rods above

catching more surfers than fish

we are getting in the way of it

today

we are living.

THIS LOVE

You can sit there

he points to the soft cushions

I smile

yes

my little heart says

this love

this is the love I need

there are two seats

one with a sarong

I saved it for you

yes

my little heart says

this love

this is how I want to be loved

he loads the surfboards on the scooter

puts my fins in without me asking

collects me

yes

this love

this is how I want to be loved

he helps

lights the candles

yes

this love

this is how I want to be loved

I glance up from doing something of little or much importance

his soft blue eyes are watching me

yes

this love

this is how I want to be loved.

I am the thinnest-skinned person I've ever met
and they tell me I must get hard
to do the work that I'm doing
but I'd rather be soft
and cry at 11:47 AM
in an airport massage chair
and then sit up
thirty minutes later
wiping tears from my eyes
and carry on with an open heart

You wouldn't understand
but I understand
and if we understand ourselves
we understand everything.

When the bombs fall

be silent

as much as you wish to raise your head

open your lungs

and yell

attack!

be silent

for this fight isn't about you

none of the fights are ever about you

just lie down

and listen to the booms

booming

until they sound very far away

and then not at all

and when you hear the dusk birds chirping

you may rise

and wash your soul of the ash.

You think you can handle me?

I have yet to meet a man with big enough hands to hold
my power and light.

Eventually you get old enough
that people can reject you
because you don't reject yourself.

IT WON'T GO AWAY

I tell him to wait

and come in September

not because I don't trust him

but because I'll feel safer then

when I hear those words leave my mouth

I'll be more comfortable then

it makes me feel like one of the first times I've chosen
myself

and not acted from a place of scarcity

not been afraid that he'll go if I say no

not been afraid that if I want some more time in between
before we fall into whatever will be fallen into

that he will be there

and if he won't be there

and he falls for a woman with the lips of summer

I trust that that's just perfect too

It's all been written in the stars anyway

perhaps this is what it feels like to trust oneself

perhaps this is what it feels like to love and respect oneself

He feels like honey in my veins

and if I've learned anything as a two-legged on this green
and blue dot

when we feel each other in the palms of our hands

and when it's to be discovered

it doesn't go away

We always fall into the hearts we are meant to know

I wish the world would wake up this Saturday

and the birds would assure them that

are you listening

darlings?

we always fall into the hearts we are meant to

and we are only held for a lifetime by those that are meant
to.

DON'T YOU EVEN COME UP HERE IF YOUR HEART SHEETS AREN'T CLEAN

I am testing him

throwing large boulders over the castle

as he climbs up

don't you even come up here if your heart sheets aren't clean

I yell

mmmmmraaaaaa!

I throw another boulder off the side of my castle

don't you show up here if you have nothing to give

mmmraaaa!

his hands grip the outside of the wall and he braces his shoulder as a boulder falls to his left

I check

he's still there

I'm only signing up to be with someone who sees

understands

and celebrates me!

I'm doing important work

special work

and not all of them have understood

and that's okay

and I love them for it

but I'm here to be celebrated

that's a non-negotiable for me

mrrraaaaaaa!

another boulder falls

so if you can't celebrate me

then just save us both some time right now

mrrrraaaaa!

my phone rings

it's not even just a phone call

it's a FaceTime

it is dark in his room

he was sleeping

I'm going to support your work

he says

I just want to know you first

so don't be vulnerable or perplexed

and go to sleep

something inside me softens

I release my fingers from the boulder

and run to the side of the castle

you look up at me and smile

as you continue to climb towards me.

I AM LOVING HIM INTO EXISTENCE

I stand in the yellow sand

feeling the wind whip between my body

I close my eyes and feel him

lately I'll do this

when I feel the absence of the love that has yet to show up

I will imagine he's already here

I'll feel the large of his hand on the small of my back

his arms coming and surprising the part of me that longs
for the tenderness of touch

I'll feel his lips on my neck as he whispers that I'm more
beautiful than the green of the Hawaiian sea

I'll feel his hand in my hand as I walk back alone

I'm getting ready to be ready for love

and sometimes in getting ready to be ready for love

we must feel the love as if it already exists

and today he is here

in the chaos of the Hawaiian sea

he is here lying on the white sheets

in the beach cottage

as I retire my brown skin naked from the sun

into his broad arms

and large smile

he is here because I am loving him into existence

and it doesn't matter when he arrives.

We sit in the sunshine

on old logs

over the dead cliffs as the yellow sunshine streams into
our cold bones and warm hearts

there is coffee in white mugs

as he speaks in English with a French accent that sounds
more like honey than the honey in my coffee

sticky and brown

and then I feel the bench vibrating with the sound of his
voice

the thrum entering my back in dance

like a song

he feels as good as he sounds.

The only way we get prepared for dying
is by living
really living
with our whole lives.

All the lights are turning green
All the lights are turning green for me.

39D

I open the blue book

but my brain

my brain cannot read

I am plagued with thoughts of you

plagues of excitement

curiosity and desire

I read sentences without reading them and keep falling
back into memories of your words and your presence

love is a cursed thing

pulling us

damning us

with the newness

it is like following a string

a string that I know by now does not always mean love

a string that can be elusive

and escape you

a string that I hear sometimes leads to the sturdy hands of
a man prepared to hold you

and so my eyes skim

dart

pupils enlarging

shrinking

as classical music dances in my ears

in 39D from Washington

and I look out at the clouds and wish to paint your face in
them

I close the book—there is no hope of my brain holding anything but the thought of you

I surrender to my utter fascination and fixation on all that you are.

I'M TRYING TO LOVE HIM LIKE A NEW DOLL

I'm trying to love him

like a new doll

a new doll that wasn't left

to have an abortion alone

because her boyfriend wouldn't sell one of his guitars to
buy a plane ticket

I'm trying to love him even though I've been left

for being too much

for 10 years

by different faces and names

left by a father who made a choice that one daughter was
enough

I'm trying to love him like the women who were never
dropped on their hearts as little girls

the ones who had nice boyfriends

who showed up on time

and opened the door

I'm trying to love him like the confident woman

who knows her worth

and sees a line of men around the corner waiting for her

so she doesn't stay up at night anxious and afraid that he
will leave her

for the flip of blonde hair from another woman with
brown legs like honey

I'm trying to love him like the light that I am
that I know that he sees

But sometimes all I am is the doll that was dropped
broken
and left on the ground

The one who has an eye that has fallen out and hangs
a button that is missing
an arm that is ripped

I am trying to love him like a new doll
but
I was a doll that was left.

Every time the train howls

I miss him

it howled before him

but in that howl I have lived in his arms

as it rushed by the tracks at night

lifting myself tiredly

from his pillows

only to find the warmth of him

and now it just howls

and I lay in bed alone

awake.

I drive by

the yellow glow

of his house

and the tears fall

we don't get to love that one

I tell my heart

but I want to

she speaks

we can love him

but he's not ours to love anymore

and with that

my blue heart and I drive down San Elijo in silence.

I woke up today with a heart that is starting to understand.

I took myself to the silver ocean at first light and crested over the top of turquoise and white waves. Body gliding, dancing, moving to the sea.

I felt a real smile—from inside.

A humpback whale covered in barnacles breached six feet away from me. A pod of dolphins came towards me—I lay quiet on my nine-foot orange longboard. Maybe they will come to me—and they did. Under and around, beside and in front. Glistening bodies, tails flying, they danced jumping into the air.

Moving through—we are all just moving through.

Baby seal bursts through the waters to peer at me—hello beautiful, I coo.

Pelicans fly and I glide against the grey and silver sky. Spirit is here amongst us. Magic is alive and beat-beating inside.

Then I found the hands and hearts of three that I love and went to the hills—the orange hills looking for the super bloom. Spring—newness, abundance, petals on petals on petals of life breaking up and through. Drinking in the rain thirsty—sip, sip, sip.

Sitting on a white blanket barefoot eating a honeycrisp apple and salami like a kid—chomp chomp.

Lying naked in a sea of orange flowers, with hair wicked and tangled from the salt of the sea. Delicate flowers caressing my legs—yellow, purple, and white blooming through.

Some people

are like being under water swimming

kicking and kicking

frantically to arrive at the surface

chest tight

oxygen gone

and then the moment your face breaks the ocean

into the world above

where birds fly

and humans sing

this feeling—is like some people.

If we

were to marry

yes, I said the M word

even though I don't think our hearts understand forever

but if you loved me—and this was important

you are important to me

so I would say yes

to you

but I would beg for no ring

I would ask you to swear at the stars

sweat in the sea

wash your pain in the rain

warm your heart with the sun

or me

to simply wake up each day

not knowing what the day will bring

and choose me.

Our bodies are paper, our kisses ink—I shall trace stories upon the lines of your hips.

Worship you with all my loving might, as the rain falls and falls and falls.

The candle dances, the coffee is cold, our bodies heat the room.

I CAN'T STOP LOOKING OVER MY SHOULDER

And all of a sudden
I can't stop
looking over my left shoulder
for your white ratty van
with the hula woman
shaking to the cream of pink across the sky
and the sound of your door slam
hard
like 70s vans are meant to
and the thud
of your feet
through the window
and that brown vest
as you lean against the doorway
with your guitar
and a smile I wanna kiss right off your face.

SUDDENLY I HAVE THE CONFIDENCE AND LEGS OF ATHENA

The hot water falls over his naked body

across a chest piece of flowers and words that mean
nothing to me

freight train jumping

sign off the road selling wild thing

I step close for a moment

pulling his body into my breasts

taking his cock gently in my hands

he stops kissing me

I have never met anyone

who turns me on so often

or so easily

and suddenly I have the confidence and legs of Athena

and the insecurity I felt over a song about another woman
falls down and runs into the drain

with every other useless thing we fall into other than love.

I'M NOT GOING TO HURT YOU

he says quietly

while my face is shoved inside the white of his t-shirt

after an hour-long conversation where I declared trust and respect and agreements and integrity

you're too perfect to hurt

he brushes my hair softly

and all the parts of me that stood on end

put their slippers on

kick back

are put to rest.

AM I THE OTHER WOMAN OR AM I FOR LIFE?

I want to hold your brown shoulders

against my white linen sheets

in my bed

I want to tear each other's body apart with nothing short
of tenderness

after a day where we have played

and lived

and loved

saved ourselves from all that is

and all that we are

and all that we aren't

and I want to rest my head

onto the beating of your heart

and for you to stay

and not just for a moment

or an hour

or a night

I would like to roll over beside you and not be surprised

but smile with all my might

because there is something pulsing through me

and the sex

and the lovemaking

and the fucking

is so good just that could make me stay till I'm grey and
my teeth are gone

but I want to make love to you in my home

in my bed

under my roof

the stars are nice

and the feeling of all of you inside of me

will stay like a sticky sweetness

but I want to make love to you

in my bed

and I want you to choose

because I can be the other woman

for a night

maybe two

but my integrity will pull me by the hair

and my self-respect will charge into my room as I sleep

and demand what we both know is right

am I the other woman?

or am I for life?

AS HIS TONGUE DOES THE WORK TONGUES WERE MEANT TO DO

And

it's really torture

that you can have a moment

like four hours of tanned thighs and limbs and tongues
and sighs till 4 in the morning

cum everywhere

bodies collapsed

clothing astray

and not meet the next day and do exactly the same

but he has another half

and I'd like to reach across my white blanket

on this green grass

and taste the purple of his lips

and the blue of his eyes

and take him inside of me

slowly

and hard

again and again

but he will need to be just one half

so I stare at his arms and see a flash of him between my
legs

hair falling as his tongue does the work tongues were
meant to do

and feel the ripple of my body for a moment before I roll
over to look at the sky.

FOR HER

No shit

she's mad

you can't lie through your teeth for five weeks

one year

who knows?

and expect a woman not to rage

I listen to her smashing buildings beneath her large green feet

roaring and taking bites off people's heads

smelling with her snout all over this city for the man whose head she wants to break so her heart can breathe and have redemption

while you run around hiding

screaming as she closes in on you

to decimate all that you are

and I'm not surprised

and I do not try to save you.

I started to send ex-lovers

men

boyfriends

a copy of my book

you're in the pages

it only makes sense

on about the tenth book, I realized I wouldn't have
enough books

to ever pull that off

on second thought

all you fuckers can just buy a copy yourself

and if you didn't make the cut

don't worry

you're in the next one.

Boundaries are the feeling of relief
you get
when you're peeing in a public bathroom
and someone wiggles the handle
the clench of anxiety in your stomach
mid-piss
wondering if you locked it
immediately met with relief
that you did
and those fuckers ain't coming in.

You're a superstar

he says

as I throw my wetsuit into a tub in my jeep

slamming the back shut

a yellow longboard hanging out the back over a red and
yellow Mexican blanket

I laugh

my breasts are still wet

drying under a sweater from 5 AM when the Californian
sun hadn't yet risen

(she's the real superstar)

I hope that's a good thing

I reply smiling

it is

he says

I have no idea what led him to that

he has never read me

I'm just a woman in a parking lot on a Monday afternoon

I let go of figuring it out

and drive off like the superstar I am.

She is a fucking looney

a straight looney toon

this world is full of looney toons

she keeps emailing and emailing

and I don't respond

all the crazies of this world just want you to be a part of their crazy

I don't have even one toe to throw into other people's crazy

I'm crazy enough.

Not all men
have balls like women.

EXPENSIVE WINE

I have been the expensive wine

who thought she was a cheap bottle of wine

for her whole life

boy

now I know that I am expensive wine

not just expensive wine

but good wine

made from grapes that have never tasted anything but the yellow roundness of the Tuscan sun

don't ask me to meet you at midnight

expensive wine doesn't meet you at midnight

it goes for breakfast

when you ask a week before

it goes for dinner

when you make a reservation

and open the goddamn door

and don't expect even a kiss

from expensive wine

because expensive wine takes time

she likes to sit

in her redness

throw it round and round

like her juicy lips

until she knows you respect her like the sun and the earth that grew her do

don't call expensive wine and tell her that you forgot she
was coming into town

when you have the attention of expensive wine

she is your world

but you didn't know you were drinking expensive wine

which is why you're going to go to sleep alone tonight

drinking cheap

sugary

shit.

HE FLIPS ME AROUND

instigating 69

with a whip of his hand

his dirty blond hair

I feel his hands grip my ass

and his tongue falls with direction between my lips

he tosses and turns my insides and I groan

taking all of him into my mouth

moving up and down his cock

I stare at the balls and wonder if all men like having their balls touched

I play and caress them

there's ass hair

or hair from somewhere right there in my face

it isn't as sexy as it is in the movies

for a moment

I think

looking at brown ass hair

brown balls

my gag reflex kicks in

I have to stop as I gag

eyes filled with water

fuck

I want this to be sexy

so sexy that five years from now you fantasize about me in bed

and then I walk down a trail of fear to a history of cheating and wonder if I don't put this dick down my throat the right way that he'll linger

and then I hate myself for that thought

and then I think about patriarchy

and how we've been sucking the dicks of this world for longer than our grandmothers can remember

and then I don't want the dick anymore

until I feel his tongue moving lovingly everywhere it should

and check back in to making love.

AS IF I AM KING KONG HERSELF

I feel the rise of vomit in my throat

I just swallowed hot cum

after 69'ing for what felt like a lifetime

we both need our jaws massaged

I get a hot flash

my eyes water

he looks at me

I run for the toilet

I let out a barf burp

from gagging on a dick with a bad gag reflex for thirty minutes

it's gone

I'm not going to throw up

thank God

and then I think about his comment on the couch earlier

I really want to see you get into it

I couldn't

it's like I freeze sometimes

I want to be sexier than I am

I want to be able to put the whole fucking dick inside my throat

like I'm sure all the other chicks do

but no

I get a third down and my eyes water

and I'm gagging and then I just feel like crying

my mom has a bad gag reflex too
always says thank god she's a lesbian

I put my hair back
with wisps of cum in it
and walk back to the bedroom
he's lying there
with a chest piece tattoo
we are new
but not so new that I cannot speak to my heart
I want to be sexier
for you
I say
I want to give you the best head you've ever had
and then when my body reacts and I can't go deeper or
farther, I wonder if there are other women who have given
you better head
and then I'm frozen in insecurity
he sits there listening
you and I have such a sexual chemistry
that technique isn't everything
he says
and I soften
because
he's right
I know we do

and I want to be more animalistic and impressive

do cool sexy moves

be a wild thing in bed

do you want that for me

or for you?

he asks

I want it for you

I reply

and I want it because I think that's what men want, or you want, or what I should do

when I think about lovemaking

he says

I'm just rolling around kissing and touching and loving you

then he starts kissing me softly

kissing away the fears and insecurities

kissing into a kiss that leads into lovemaking where our knees do not shake and I shake the bed as if I am King Kong herself.

They say forgiveness heals ourselves

but sometimes I just like to make those motherfuckers
pay.

How funny is it that the work

in a relationship

when we are betrayed

to move on

to let go

to forgive

is our own?

Shouldn't those fuckers get the work?

it's like we get fucked twice

fucked with a lie

and then fucked with a job to feel secure every time his
phone dies at a bar

every time he has eyes or ears for a woman

every time he comes home late

every time it gets hard

it's my job

to trust

it's like pulling the short end of the stick

twice

I think the universe got this all wrong.

She is prancing with blonde hair

and a white dress

the light turns green

and she runs

but she falls

tripping on the cement with bare feet

and falls to the ground

tears falling a little late

as kids' tears do

her dad swoops her up

in his arms

and holds her high

she is crying and fighting a little

as he crosses the street

what a gift to be held like that

what a gift to be loved like that.

The morning light leaps through his eyelashes

I love even them

they begin black like the night

and then curl into a white

as if the sunshine inside of him has penetrated through
his body

and is seeping from his eyes

they are green and dance and sparkle

and the words fall away

while I have a love story with each eyelash and each
pigment of color in his eyes.

THE SENSUALITY LIVING INSIDE OF ME
STRETCHES

We feel the heat

it's the same heat we felt

against the wall of the bar

except there is no blackness now

no guilt

it's just to be tasted

and we are to be destroyed

by the limbs and yellow arms

and pink lips

I feel his tongue running circles inside my mouth

my eyes close

on a roller coaster Ferris wheel

the Sensuality living inside of me stretches

opens one eye with a grin

that only the devil knows what it feels like

she is naked

with the arm of a leftover lover

across the flesh of her ass

she lifts his arm

lights a cigarette

blows white smoke into the blackness

and wakes him up to begin again

I take my hands in broad daylight and run them over the
lines of his penis in his blue jeans

our tongues still dancing

the world spins and spins

hazy and fading in the broad daylight

I feel his tongue moving on my neck

his strong fingers saying hello to the purple of my nipples
in the mountain air

surrounded by the desert

she doesn't care

we heave our bodies into the tent

and it is between those two broad arms

rippling with me inside of them

juices flying

wetness roaring

hair being pulled from its roots

sensuality inside of me screams

I take him strongly

feel the flesh of his perfect ass in my palms

his shaft moving in and out and in and out and in and out
inside of me

my back feels the roots and rocks of this world

but we keep going

Sensuality is cheering

her lover wakes up from her bed

asks what's the ruckus

she shushes him and opens her ears and arms to the
experience pulsing through my veins

I am so wet that his dick floats inside effortlessly

out in the air

inside

hovering with just the tip teasing me

I bite his ear hoarsely and want to scream

deeper

slowly

fast

his hips moving like a freight train to Georgia

my ass bouncing below him

feeling the flesh of his balls

rubbing my clit with saliva in circles

bodies scream

I open the lungs

the choir raises its hands

trumpets bellow

cellos groan

guitars rip

while the hair sways and eyes close

body pulsing

gasping into the sweetness and surrender of the unknown

we lie limp

arms astray

minds astray

all feeling

shaking at the slightest sigh

fingers trace in the red light of the afternoon glow

we should be doing

yet we are being

we have been

I lie down beside Sensuality and light a cigarette

my body making the mattress bounce

how was that?

I ask over the whiteness of my chest

getting better

she says

I walk barefoot, blue jeans around my hips

leaving the mellow notes of the guitar in the distance

as the sun shines on my face.

WHEN PEOPLE GET ANGRY READING YOUR WRITING

you know you're doing it right

for what they are really saying is, "How dare you!"

they do not understand that we all have a truth

there are a million truths in this world

none more right than the next

keep writing

do not be afraid to speak

step on all the toes you want

if someone chooses to be insulted by your words

so be it

their anger is a reflection of their miserable lives

staring them in the face

through your pen.

SOMEONE HAS TO WRITE HALLMARK FLUFF

sappy ass-wipe for lemmings
mass-produced, tasteless, comfortable conditioned truth
they need that, too

Someone has to write from the core
the core isn't always pretty
No
it doesn't always say please, thank you, are you ready?
it says the things we don't say out loud
the things that enrage
cause upheaval
trigger and pull
words that are shoved down non-lubricated minds
as they yell, "Wait! Wait!"

So let's all keep writing
say it all out loud
feed the world what it wants
and doesn't want
there's room for all of us here.

IL BURRO

the Italians yell

but only in the south

your body is like butter!

in Canada—imbeciles yelling shit

and not only this—no

he makes pasta

tasting like Jesus

from tomates y azucar

eats with the serving spoon

What!

he yells

there is no more spoons

bottles caked in wax

wine in coffee cups

yes—this is a gentleman

I'm moving to Italy.

How old are you?
I ask
old enough to take care of you
he replies.

THERE ARE NO NEW GREATS

there hasn't been writing worth reading

in years

yes, there are good writers—but no greats

why?

maybe because we write lists

top 5 ways to make her scream

10 ways to know if he's cheating on you

7 things real yogis do

this isn't writing

this isn't talent

this is click-hungry publications

publishing absolute garbage

devoured by a generation

with the attention span of gerbils

some of it is so goddamn bad it makes me want to pull my
teeth out

how it's read and loved is beyond me

Maybe if we watched less television

stared at the stars

we would write

something worth reading

but we don't even look at the stars

and don't send me the mushroom trip you wrote about
your ex-girlfriend

it's not writing

it's not poetry

it's complete and utter crap and I hate it

we need delayed gratification

we need blood and sweat and words that scream from the core

all else is shit.

I wish to sink my teeth

into the tired soul of the world

man meditating amongst vultures at sunset

I lie on my back

watch the sky

with all my eyes

smooth tips ripple like muscle

in the sunlight

not the sunlight that beats down unwanted and hot

but the sunlight that warms the sky pink

like those flowers covered in dust

as I walk up the sullen hill.

Patience

he says

this is not a sprint

it's a marathon

I'm more of a hundred-meter sprinter

I reply.

SUDDENLY THE THANKS MAKE SENSE

I read a poem

by a poet I do not know

and the first five lines

grabbed my insides and answered a why

I didn't know needed answering

and all of a sudden

I get why

my simple musings on life

that I do not find extraordinary (that others find
extraordinary)

I for a moment get why they write me

thanking me profusely

for something I don't find so brilliant

or profound

or worth noting

or thanking

it is

extraordinary

for we are all looking for those five lines

to know why (we are the same).

Yes

and there are other days

where I walk so tall

my hair scratches God's ass

there are days where I love myself so mightily

people resent me for the love they forget to give
themselves

there are days where I have to whack my self-esteem down

with large heavy pounds

for the arrogance that lives in all of us

has come out breathing fire

we all have all of it inside of us.

Which ones are the best?

I ask him

he stares out into the night

the ones that haven't been created yet.

Sometimes I straight up share the poems I write about them too soon

just to see if they are chickenshits

and will run away from the word love

it's a good defense mechanism

I can hide behind being a poet

with pretty words

refusing to be vulnerable

and write a poem about smacking their scared asses on the way out

except I'm scared

which is why I see if they

will

run

first.

I WILL REMEMBER ECUADOR

as logs of palo santo the size of my left arm

burning through the night

walking through the streets

the musk of palo santo everywhere

brown mud squeezing through my big toes

red scratches on large white mosquito bites

black sand flies

a brown ocean

dogs playing deeply

the musk of rain and red-hot sunsets

waves the size of Jesus crashing toward me in the silver
and pink light of last light

the tongues of lovers who know the lips of women that
move with a non-urgency that is sacred

red feet burning on sand when the sun is full and hot

small green pathways to beaches

statues of great mighty rocks that demand respect

statues of warriors guarding abandoned buildings
destroyed by hurricanes and this life

I will remember Ecuador as everything she is and
everything I do not know yet.

Just remember that you're wanted, and you've been wanted since the moment you were born.

Every single person on this planet is gifted by your presence.

And the healing is not in understanding that you are wanted externally—it's deeper; the work is wanting yourself.

Wanting yourself is the key to the door you do not know needs to be opened.

Deeply wanting yourself so fully and really that you abandon the need to be wanted externally and fall into a security that is unshakable inside.

This is the work that your heart is begging you for.

STOP MAKING IT ABOUT YOU

it was never about you

this life is never personal

we just don't know how to exist

without attachment to ourselves

go on

it is and always has been outside of you.

He stands there in a grey t-shirt
bald head
holding a coffee cup
with some worn-down logo etched on its side
suddenly a large black Bernese mountain dog
saunters slowly towards him
like a bear
on no leash
and they walk
slowly
him drinking his coffee
four paws behind
that is exactly the life I want.

And the same dad

that we saw

waving his hands

wildly and arrogantly

as he talked about sports

is suddenly on his knees

on the red carpet

in the Fairmont

with hair a mess

collecting the purple and orange Cheerios of his son

while the mother drinks her coffee

exhausted and frazzled

and then I forgive him

and love him in a heartbeat

to be human.

And she goes

turn your heart off

I am stunned

like a deer in headlights

I wish to never live a day in my life with my heart turned
off

detachment is beautiful

however, my sadness is my guru

my happiness my god

my insecurity my teacher

my arrogance my guide

my emotions are the gifts of my life

how dare you

ask me to turn them off?

A GOOD ARTIST DOESN'T HAVE EARS, ONLY EYES AND A THROAT TO SPEAK

You have social obligation

responsibility

you have to watch your mouth

I spit my coffee out

oh!

I'm sorry—you thought my art was about you?

you thought I am sitting in a room pouring all that I am onto paper for you?

I let out a mad laugh

and you're here to try and put me back in the box that I write to leave?

you're here to tell the artist who is trying not to conform with her voice

to conform?

another laugh

what other brilliant advice do you have for me?

that I'm on a pedestal?

that because I'm a celebrity

that I have to set a good example for them nice young girls?

I hope them nice young girls read my art and feel the fire in their belly begin to burn that they will need to live

and I hope the people who pull at the non-conformists to conform

because they're uncomfortable seeing someone do it another way

seeing someone find belonging not through a herd of
sheep

but through their dharma

rot in the hell of their comfortability

a good artist doesn't have ears

only eyes

and a throat to speak.

CAN YOU NOT WRITE ABOUT ME?

they ask

you might as well ask me if I can not breathe for the rest of my life

the answer is no

I must write about you

for every poem is about a you

of sorts

and if I stop writing about you

I stop writing at all

and I cannot do that

for this is my life's calling

my life is the material of my work

and it really isn't about you

you are an impression

a moment of my truth

a thing in a story

passing in the wind in between the last poem I wrote and the poem I have yet to start

it is only about you to the yous who know I speak of you

one person

the other hundred thousand

the other million

they don't know it's you

and a poem will never be the whole truth

no

that's impossible

horseshit

of course not

it's my truth

don't ask me to take it down

or alter it to be more true

to capture the whole story

art is subjective, idiot

and good art is never neutral

it doesn't open the door for you

ask how you like your steak cooked

it bites with a truth that is only from one and for one—me

if you want to share your truth

write it yourself

I respect you by not naming you

respect me by never again asking me to remove my art.

IT'S NOT ABOUT VEGANS

Of course, it's not about vegans

fuckwits

it's about condescending

self-righteous

shitheads

who grab a thing by the balls

and then diss anyone who doesn't like those same balls in
their mouth

and take every chance they can

with their bumper stickers

and their t-shirts

and their loud yapping mouths

that having certain balls in their mouth is better than yours

tofu balls

tempeh balls

seitan balls

saving the planet

blah, blah

balls

I'm just writing

to say

I don't care what kind of balls are in your mouth

if you must stop and take the time to tell me

I think you're an asshole

and that's it.

DO NOT PRAISE ME FOR MY SUFFERING

Hear me for my suffering

find redemption from my suffering

have respect for my suffering

connect to my suffering—we all suffer

but do not praise me for my suffering

do not know me

just

for

my suffering

know me for my words that cut like fire

and my heart that melts ice

my presence that is warm like the buzz of a honeybee to
pink petals who want it near

know me for my brash humor

my wit that cuts

my insecurity that shakes when it walks into a room of
greats

turns to the man beside me

to ask

do I belong?

but lord I hope I never become famous

or known

for my suffering

even be it my honesty in suffering

for I know it is rare in a world that shuts its blinds

and locks out the world when they are not well

and walks out Monday with shining white-stained perfect teeth

and a white Starbucks mug

not a hair amiss

yelling

"Hi Joe!"

sweetly and surely

as you drive by waving

but

I don't want to spread that message

suffering

no, suffering is not my message

honesty is easy

honesty is also not my message

I want to be remembered for my heart

for the words I draw

that dance

of what it means to be human

so when people say

thank you when I share my pain

a part of me cringes

because I hope you see more than my pain or my suffering or my honesty

I hope that why I wake and create shines through and you remember me for that.

YOU CANNOT BE DEPRESSED WHEN YOU ARE GRATEFUL

You cannot be depressed
when you are grateful
his words exit the -3 degree Celsius air
and freeze the world around me
that's it
that's the key
the key to the problem
I may never solve
but try
for we do not save them
people save themselves
or they stop
and we just pray
they don't stop themselves
but we can guide them
guiding them is my part-time job
and I will no longer do it
sitting with depression in the chair next to me
I will do it
ripping in a small plane
through a field of yellow wheat at dusk
with her in the passenger seat
eyes gleaming
as we take off

into the sky

and move

up

up

up

and circle around the purple lupins

and the mountains that are blue and cold

and the engine in this thing

roars in the cold

and her eyes are wide

in gratitude

as she digests the geese flying south

and the cows like small specks below

and the pink sky as the sun waves her last goodbye wildly

and suddenly

depression is so far away

yelling to be heard

but she cannot hear it

for all she can feel in her heart

is joy

and that

is how we heal it

my brain finishes.

Suddenly

life feels less warm

and I realize

it is all about the people

these tundras contain empty space and silence

and a beauty I understand in a way I didn't know that I
needed

but without the warm heartbeats of those we love

this world is empty

I wish to find more of those same heartbeats

to take shelter and joy in

perhaps

that's really the point.

I want to be
the lioness
that he knows.

THE FLOWERS DID NOT BEAR THE HONEY
THAT YOU ARE

You're like sunshine in a glass bottle

and I wish to be trapped in between the gentle
movements of your hips

but not until

I first

land softly in the right side of your heart

that is so built for loving

You love this world with a weight that is rare

it is not often I meet somebody equipped to love this
world

harder

and softer than I

you are the connectedness I could not find

the flowers did not bear the honey that you are

the sky did not bear the clouds that provide the shade that
I need

You are the shelter from the wind that I wasn't ready for

the warmth I seek

in hands I found by accident

But your fingers are cut off from a love that is not loving

and as I reach for you

I fall into the sweetness and knowingness of all that you
are

alone

yet I discover you here (for now)

I hope one day to kiss

softly

the edge of each of your fingers and sink into you

sink into the broadness of your back

the softness in your chest

the pink of your tongue

to wake with the blond of your hair on a pillow beside me

make you a dark strong coffee

while you lie in white sheets

and seize the day with the joy you and I share in our
bones and hearts and sparkling eyes

You feel like the green sea hitting my body after
wandering parched

through the African desert

for weeks.

You are in these pages

but you wouldn't know

for you left the poems I wrote about you

folded

on paper

with black ink

on the corner of the bedside table

untouched

and then you left them there all night

for a week

maybe that was the first time I should have known it
wouldn't be long until you left me.

Women would be less angry
if men had more courage.

THIS INTIMACY

is something I have only read about

not touched with the blue and grey of my eyes

you

I touch you

in the night light

with eyelashes that only shut to breathe

and we just lay there

song after song after song

staring at one another

your head resting in the bed of your elbow

and the tears fall

softly down my cheeks

like the salty pieces of unconditional love that is pulsing
through my heart

it as if I have walked for 10,000 miles without the gift of
my eyes

just the sense of my feet

the wetness of my tongue

and then suddenly my eyes have sprouted from my heart

and all there is

is you

I believe our eyes are our hearts

not the windows to our soul

our souls float

not in our chests

It takes everything in me to look away
from a moment I've been avoiding my entire life
this presence
is why we roam the earth thirsty and hungry
and it is what we so rarely feed ourselves

This morning I am still holding the blue
and two golden specks in your eyes
in my chest
this will forever be etched in sacredness in my heart.

I once dated a man briefly
who told me that I was a piece of gold
that he had to leave on the pavement
and that pieces of gold
don't stay
sitting on the pavement
unclaimed
for long.

The last sentence is the best

he says

I write the whole thing

for the last sentence

I say

everything else is foreplay.

DON'T FUCK THE MESSENGER (OR DO)

I'm glad you finally found the froth

he says

I think that the universe has been trying to tell me for a
while

but I got confused

and thought it was okay to fuck surfers

instead.

FOR FUCK'S SAKE DON'T BE NEUTRAL

don't just be empathetic with somebody's side

to be well liked

to show you understand all sides

of course you understand all sides

it's why you stood tall

and stood where you are

being neutral kills everything

it kills our spirit

it kills our art

it kills our marriages

have a fucking opinion

and yell it from the rooftops

your lungs are here to be abused with passion

your brain is here to manipulate you every day and
sometimes have something worth saying

neutrality is the devil

stand where you wish to stand.

THE SOLUTION ISN'T
women covering their legs
that doesn't reprogram the parts of us
that have been mass-conditioned to think
the female body means sex
the solution is
why do we believe what we believe?
and can we believe differently?

SOME WOMEN HAVE BECOME SO HARDENED
BY THIS PATRIARCHAL WORLD

that I have no interest in cracking them

it's all a front

this masculine bravado

this one of the boys

it is all the tail of a scorpion that has been burned by a
world that leads us to think that sensitivity is a weakness

and emotional is exhausting

so we suffocate our femininity

we morph into the men who need our softness the most

and their masculine shells convince some

oh

she is strong

we think

but I see through their layers

not like that, I think

not like that

their layers are thorns of suppressed roses that need
healing

their fronting a defense mechanism so deep

so unconscious

they have no idea that they are terrified to be vulnerable

to be open

to be emotional

to be sensitive

so they put on the only energy they can find to survive in

this world

I have no interest

in cracking these women

for their thorns run deep

and their softness is their own to find.

You're not broken

your pieces are just resting.

TO THE WOMEN WHO LACKED THE HANDS TO HOLD ME

It is like a lightbulb of betrayal going off in my soul
one by one
I see the moments as they are
women that I love
not holding me up
but punching me in the soul

Perhaps they wish to take the shine
that I cherish and openly worship inside of them
from me
they do not know it is theirs
too
perhaps they didn't know
but I am suddenly looking at their unconscious Joker
who is laughing
evilly
as it all comes to

He has white paint around his eyes
red lips
a hat with three dangling bells
oh
yes
I was manipulating you
he walks around me slowly

madly

falling and laughing

large laughs that echo off the dark walls of my psyche

you didn't even know it was happening!

laughs

you thought I was your friend!

he is drifting a feather across my shoulder as he speaks
slowly into my ear

Their faces flash in front of me

all of them

they dance across my brain

recounting

recognizing

I see them all for what they are

I lash out and scream

elbow the Joker in the face

I look at him and scream again

feeling my power reclaim itself in my belly

feeling my intuition fill and fill and fill

feeling my feet

sturdy in the ground

as the Joker stands below me

laughing

holding his bleeding lip
I step over him
and her
and her
and her
and her
into all that I am.

I'd like to negotiate periods
with God.

I show him the cover of my last book

that is definitely going to sell

he says

women are angry

that is why I just hide in my house all day.

Seize the salt, seize the ones you wish to kiss with your whole heart. Seize the sunshine as it rolls through the heavens onto your cheeks, seize the warmth of a coffee at sunrise when the ground still holds the chill of the night.

Seize the gratitude in the Englishman who paddles beside you with greys that know of more waves than you've seen.

Seize that thing that calls you to contribute to it when you are listening quietly to nobody's heart but the one thumping in your chest.

Seize the first moments of the day, not with your phone or your laptop but with a fistful of hair and the mouth of the gorgeous human existing beside you.

Seize this life—I beg of you to do nothing else.

What a gift that each morning the sun reaches for us all—
without us ever asking or thanking her for her life.

What a gift that every night, the moon rises to blanket the
night's sky so the stars may dance on their left toes and
then their right.

What a gift that we may exist between it all, between the
heartbeats at first light, that we may be nourished by the
salt, the two-leggeds, and the four-leggeds.

I wish to never wake from this life I am living—it is so
beautiful that it cracks my heart open fresh with sweet
might.

I SAID I LOVE YOU YESTERDAY

for the first time in years

how many years you ask

maybe eight

maybe never

maybe eight years ago I didn't even know what love means

do we ever really know what love means?

the moment we fall out of love

we doubt that we were ever in love

and some argue that love is only love if it's internal

I argue

hanging over the bed in the candlelight

that's like giving someone a candy

and then taking it back

you have to love the ones you've loved

even if you aren't in love with them anymore

his blond hair hangs off the bed across from me

it's been five minutes since we said our first love-yous

and I'm already grilling him about whether it means
anything

whether I mean anything

whether his words have weight

if this I love you has weight

I sit staring at him with our heads kind of hanging off the
bed for a good twenty minutes

or six songs

before the words came out

they got stuck

they've been living inside my forehead having tea with my brain and arguing for weeks

about whether it's too soon

or if it's really love!

because who the fuck knows

it's been so long really

and the last man I was falling in love with

racing through a field at dusk

running my hands through yellow wheat

that man said it wasn't possible

that I couldn't possibly be in love after five weeks

and then he ended it

and I've coached clients through this

I love him

but it hasn't been three months

why do you have to wait three months?

because that's the amount of time you have to wait before you tell someone you love them

they say

oh

I reply

smiling

who made that rule?

I lovingly mocked their rules and gently coaxed those three words from their throats

till they felt freedom

yet here I am

head hanging off the bed

like a fool

songs flipping by

and the moments never right

I want him to be looking at me

I want to see his eyes

I want the perfect song

and then the words get stuck

when it's right and I just stare at him

thinking the words free in my head

wishing someone would crawl inside my throat and pull them by the tail

as they screech and holler

running with big scaly feet back down my throat

ah!

they yell

it isn't safe!

what the fuck happens once we come out?

too much pressure!

then it must be forever!

what if you don't even know what love means and this is infatuation or just really strong like

maybe it's just really strong like!

and then you're lying!

the inner dialogue runs through my brain

after about four songs he looks at me perplexed

should I be concerned?

he thinks I'm pregnant

or leaving

now I've really fucked up the moment

no!

I squirm

I think I might love you

oh

he says

smiling

I knew it!

I knew it!

I think I might love you too

he says grabbing my face and pulling all of me inside

and then my whole body goes into shock

because when I said I fall in love fast a month ago

he said it took him longer

and it's only been five weeks

and I expected to just love him for a good six months or a
year and wait for those three words

I expected a stone silence

a thanks

a kiss and then quiet

but there they are

all the monsters hiding in our brains drinking champagne
together

And when we are lying together

after we've said I love you

and I've argued whether his I love you is real

just to be sure

safe

you know?

and after we've made love

and my body has fallen apart around me

and we're lying there

him sleeping on his back

me trying to fire off an email at 1:30 AM

that I don't give a fuck about because I just want to be in
love

but I also have integrity on steroids

I want to shake him awake a little

I want to say those three words alone

not with I might

so I go pee

and take my clothes off really clumsy and loud

snoring

get into the bed, throwing my weight into the bed

snoring

yanking the covers in hopes he'll crack an eye

snoring

so I lean over

and whisper quietly

I love you

goodnight

And when we wake up in the morning

I think it will be different

but it's the same

and we drink our coffee and I don't wish to announce it to anyone

I just want to stew on it

and in it

and feel it through.

The best sex I've ever had is when we get to know the soul first.

Where the heart and person feel like home before we've undressed and then we know where the kitchen is and the sandwich stuff and can make whatever sandwich we want without worrying about where the mustard is or the knives live.

Where our souls have enough time to intermingle and swap vulnerability chickenshits—where our biggest fears within intimacy come out roaring and ugly, and we get to sit and have tea with them, and decide the monsters aren't really that scary after all, and choose to stay.

And in that stayingness, undress deeper and deeper and deeper until we are able to reach a cavity so deep in our hearts and bodies that the physical intimacy is just a mirror of the intimacy we reached earlier—with naked, dripping, wet, vulnerable souls.

Your wildness was never meant to be kept in a cage.

I know that sometimes they tell you that. They tell you that because they're so damn afraid of what would happen if they were free.

If they were free they would tear their suit off like a tiger, throw their paperwork around the room like monkeys, jump and roam and scream.

This world would go mad for a moment, for so many of us don't know what it means to be free.

We think being free is getting wasted and doing twenty shots on a Friday to mask and numb the lives we hate—poisoning our body with excuses for why we can't quit it all. We think freedom is lines of cocaine, where we can live in a different plane.

You escape because you believe you are trapped, and you have trapped yourself, wild child.

It's inside of you—growling and begging to be let loose so you may honor your truth. Break free and be.

Watching you

is like watching someone turn

water

into wine

he says.

I spread my legs wide in my black tights

my brown corduroy skirt opening

thigh wide

it feels nice

free

like I'm doing something I shouldn't

mmm

like the confidence after the vulnerability

like the lips of your vagina breathing in the daylight for a moment

sinning without sinning because it's how we were always born to be

It's so nice wearing a skirt with tights

because you can just spread eagle

I say into the space

you're not the kind of woman that seems good at keeping your legs closed

he replies

wait

laughing

well

you know what I mean.

I love you

I say with my eyes

he stares at me

eyes half open

green in the morning light

I smile inside

I love you

I say again

from a place that he'll never know or hear or understand

I love you

I say

with my eyes

smiling a little on the outside

he is reading me

but he cannot hear those words

all he sees is the sparkle in my eyes

it's the best secret I've ever kept.

His green eyes freeze

against my woven bed frame

I wonder for a moment why we don't just spend our
entire lives staring into the eyes of our lovers

without speaking

with anything but our eyes

for the rest of our lives

In those eyes I am safe

in those eyes I am found

And maybe

I've been safe and found all along

and I just needed those green eyes to listen.

PERHAPS MY GREATEST LOVER WAS I

I wake up hot

it's already reaching for the 30s

my soft body feels the sheets and is aroused by the way they
bend and fold

the energy inside of me is dancing and she wants to be
touched and felt

I start slowly

putting pressure with my hand—not using my fingers—
just letting her know I'm there

and then I begin to touch her

slowly

she gets wet quickly

I dreamt of my body being taken

being bounced up and down

on the shaft of a man

climaxing in my dreams

I touch my clitoris awake but don't stay long

I want to go deep inside

I prop my hips up on a pillow

2 fingers slide inside

I touch deep

deep back inside

it is wet and warm and I start to slowly drum

drumming and massage

slowly in the morning light

I moan

massaging and moving my hand outside

it is wet

soaking my clitoris

I play with her for a little while

but not long

before

I dive deep inside again

thrusting and drumming my hand inside my cavity

I begin to lose myself

I imagine that my fingers are a shaft of a lover

I kiss my left arm wetly and with passion

drumming inside

feeling outside

wetness exploding between my brown thighs

spilling onto the sheets

drenching my underwear

I am consumed

tired

panting

20 minutes goes by

teasing climax

slowing down

re-entering

finally I fall

from the mountains

moaning

my body shakes

falls apart as if the greatest lover has just spent hours
between my legs

perhaps my greatest lover is I.

Blunt, raw, and immediately accessible emotionally, intellectually, and spiritually to all who read her words, Janne Robinson is a societal visionary, counterculture poet, film director, retreat leader, workshop lecturer, and truth coach who swings from the very first sentence. Robinson's work as an artist and facilitator is to encourage people to become accessible to their truths. She believes that our world is sick—and truth is our medicine.

Janne stumbled upon the fierceness of her poetry in "This is for the women who don't give a fuck," written in 2015. The poem grew teeth and ran through the world—capturing the eyes and hearts of millions of women thirsty for their power. She later went on to create and self-direct films of her poems, *This is for the women who don't give a fuck, I will never be a well-behaved woman,* and *I am a woman of distinction,* all garnering critical acclaim.

She released her first book and collection of poetry, *This Is for the Women Who Don't Give a Fuck,* in 2017 while simultaneously building "This is for the women," a media and apparel brand that empowers women to walk tall like an old cypress tree. In every medium Robinson has explored, she has given voice and a strength to dream to both women and men no longer willing to live by the constraints of established norms.

She has become a herald for whom the phrases "walk tall" and "take up space" are multidimensional breakthroughs, at a time when women are owning their voices and challenging ideals set by society. Her words blend aspects of Allen Ginsberg, Mary Oliver, and Anaïs Nin, combining social commentary with natural images and matter-of-fact sexuality. Her words pointedly express disdain for conformity and champion a commitment to expansive self-discovery.

Unpolitically correct and brazenly honest, Janne Robinson walks in with a confidence that shakes the knees of those still learning how to define themselves and leaves us with hope and a greater understanding of ourselves and it all.